Philip Larkin

Philip Larkin is recognised as one of the most important writers to have emerged in Britain since the Second World War. First published in 1982, Andrew Motion's study begins with an account of Larkin's life and literary background and discusses his literary relationship with Hardy and Yeats and his association with the Movement. He analyses Larkin's two novels and assesses his three mature collections. Throughout the book much reference is made to uncollected reviews and articles and occasionally to unpublished manuscripts. Rather than developing the familiar line on Larkin as an empirical and melancholy writer, Andrew Motion explores the Symbolist and transcendent element in his work, and emphasises its range and variety.

Philip Larkin

Andrew Motion

Routledge
Taylor & Francis Group

First published in 1982
by Methuen & Co. Ltd

This edition first published in 2010 by Routledge
2 Park Square, Milton Park, Abingdon, Oxon, OX14 4RN

Simultaneously published in the USA and Canada
by Routledge
270 Madison Avenue, New York, NY 10016

Routledge is an imprint of the Taylor & Francis Group, an informa business

© 1982 Andrew Motion

Publisher's Note
The publisher has gone to great lengths to ensure the quality of this
reprint but points out that some imperfections in the original copies may
be apparent.

Disclaimer
The publisher has made every effort to trace copyright holders and
welcomes correspondence from those they have been unable to contact.

ISBN 13: 978-0-415-56243-0 (hbk)

ISBN 10: 0-415-56243-0 (hbk)

PHILIP
LARKIN

ANDREW MOTION

METHUEN
LONDON AND NEW YORK

First published in 1982 by
Methuen & Co. Ltd
11 New Fetter Lane, London EC4P 4EE
Published in the USA by
Methuen & Co.
in association with Methuen, Inc.
733 Third Avenue, New York, NY 10017

© *1982 Andrew Motion*

Typeset by Rowland Phototypesetting Ltd
Printed in Great Britain by
Richard Clay (The Chaucer Press) Ltd
Bungay, Suffolk

British Library Cataloguing in Publication Data

Motion, Andrew
Philip Larkin. – (Contemporary writers)
1. Larkin, Philip – Criticism and interpretation
I. Title   II. Series
828'.914   PR6023.A66Z/
ISBN 0-416-32270-0

Library of Congress Cataloging in Publication Data

Motion, Andrew, 1952–
Philip Larkin.
(Contemporary writers)
Bibliography: p.
1. Larkin, Philip – Criticism and interpretation.
I. Title.   II. Series.
PR6023.A66Z77   1982   821'.914   82-7988
ISBN 0-416-32270-0 (pbk.)   AACR2

CONTENTS

GENERAL EDITORS' PREFACE

Over the past twenty years or so, it has become clear that a decisive change has taken place in the spirit and character of contemporary writing. There now exists around us, in fiction, drama and poetry, a major achievement which belongs to our experience, our doubts and uncertainties, our ways of perceiving – an achievement stylistically radical and novel, and likely to be regarded as quite as exciting, important and innovative as that of any previous period. This is a consciousness and a confidence that has grown very slowly. In the 1950s it seemed that, somewhere amidst the dark realities of the Second World War, the great modernist impulse of the early years of this century had exhausted itself, and that the post-war arts would be arts of recessiveness, pale imitation, relative sterility. Some, indeed, doubted the ability of literature to survive the experiences of holocaust. A few major figures seemed to exist, but not a style or a direction. By the 1960s the confidence was greater, the sense of an avant-garde returned, the talents multiplied, and there was a growing hunger to define the appropriate styles, tendencies and forms of a new time. And by the 1970s it was not hard to see that we were now surrounded by a remarkable, plural, innovative generation, indeed several layers of generations, whose works represented a radical inquiry into contemporary forms and required us to read and understand – or, often, to read and *not* understand – in quite new ways. Today, as the 1980s start, that cumulative post-war achievement has acquired a degree of coherence that allows for critical response and understanding; hence the present series.

We thus start it in the conviction that the age of Beckett, Borges, Nabokov, Bellow, Pynchon, Robbe-Grillet, Golding, Murdoch, Fowles, Grass, Handke and Calvino, of Albee, Mamet, Shepard, Ionesco, Orton, Pinter and Stoppard, of Ginsberg, Lowell, Ashbery, Paz, Larkin and Hughes, and many another, is indeed an outstanding age of international creation, striking experiment, and some degree of aesthetic coherence. It is a time that has been described as 'post-modern', in the sense that it is an era consequent to modernism yet different from it, having its own distinctive preoccupations and stylistic choices. That term has its limitations, because it is apt to generate too precise definitions of the contemporary experiment, and has acquired rather too specific associations with contemporary American writing; but it does help concentrate our sense of living in a distinctive period. With the new writing has come a new criticism or rather a new critical theorem, its thrust being 'structuralist' or 'deconstructive' – a theorem that not only coexists with but has affected that writing (to the point where many of the best theorists write fictions, the best fictionalists write criticism). Again, its theory can be hermetic and enclosing, if not profoundly apocalyptic; but it points to the presence in our time of a new sense of the status of word and text, author and reader, which shapes and structures the making of modern form.

The aim of 'Contemporary Writers' is to consider some of the most important figures in this scene, looking from the standpoint of and at the achievement of the writers themselves. Its aims are eclectic, and it will follow no tight definition of the contemporary; it will function on the assumption that contemporary writing is by its nature multidirectional and elusive, since styles and directions keep constantly changing in writers who, unlike the writers of the past, are continuous, incomplete, not dead (though several of these studies will address the careers of those who, though dead, remain our contemporaries, as many of those who continue to write are manifestly

7

not). A fair criticism of living writers must be assertive but also provisional, just as a fair sense of contemporary style must be open to that most crucial of contemporary awarenesses, that of the suddenness of change. We do not assume, then, that there is one right path to contemporary experiment, nor that a self-conscious reflexiveness, a deconstructive strategy, an art of performance or a metafictional mode is the only one of current importance. As Iris Murdoch said, 'a strong agile realism which is of course not photographic naturalism' – associated perhaps especially with British writing, but also with Latin-American and American – is also a major component of modern style.

So in this series we wish to identify major writers, some of whom are avant-garde, others who are familiar, even popular, but all of whom are in some serious sense contemporary and in some contemporary sense serious. The aim is to offer brief, lucid studies of their work which draw on modern theoretical issues but respond, as much modern criticism does not, to their distinctiveness and individual interest. We have looked for contributors who are engaged with their subjects – some of them being significant practising authors themselves, writing out of creative experience, others of whom are critics whose interest is personal as well as theoretical. Each volume will provide a thorough account of the author's work so far, a solid bibliography, a personal judgement – and, we hope, an enlarged understanding of writers who are important, not only because of the individual force of their work, but because they are ours in ways no past writer could really be.

Norwich, England, 1981   MALCOLM BRADBURY
                                 CHRISTOPHER BIGSBY

ACKNOWLEDGEMENTS

I am very grateful to Philip Larkin for the generous help and advice he gave me while I was writing this book, and for his permission to quote from his manuscript notebook (Add. MS 52,619) in the British Library.

A number of other people have also given me their help, and my particular thanks are due to Gay Clifford, Barbara Everett, Alan Hollinghurst, Blake Morrison, Joanna Jane Motion, Craig Raine and Tracey Warr. I should also like to thank the Bodleian Library, Oxford, and the Department of Manuscripts of the British Library for their assistance.

The author and publisher would like to thank the following for permission to reproduce copyright material: Faber & Faber Ltd for extracts from *The North Ship* and *The Whitsun Weddings* by Philip Larkin; Faber & Faber Ltd and Farrar, Straus & Giroux, Inc. for extracts from *High Windows* by Philip Larkin; Faber & Faber Ltd and The Overlook Press for extracts from *Jill* and *A Girl in Winter* by Philip Larkin; The Marvell Press for extracts from *The Less Deceived* by Philip Larkin; The Sycamore Press and Philip Larkin for 'Femmes Damnées'; Philip Larkin for 'Aubade', first published in *The Times Literary Supplement* (December 1977).

A NOTE ON THE TEXTS

Except where indicated in the Notes, quotations from works by Philip Larkin are taken from the editions listed below. The following abbreviations have been used:

AWJ *All What Jazz: A Record Diary 1961–68* (London: Faber, 1970)

GW *A Girl in Winter*, 1st paperback edn (London: Faber, 1975)

HW *High Windows* (London: Faber, 1974)

J *Jill*, 1st paperback edn (London: Faber, 1975)

LD *The Less Deceived* (London: Marvell Press, 1955)

NS *The North Ship*, 2nd edn (London: Faber, 1966)

WW *The Whitsun Weddings* (London: Faber, 1964)

1

INTRODUCTION

It is hard to write a critical book on Philip Larkin without feeling guilty. He has surrounded the approach to his poems with complaints that academics and students destroy the relationship between literature and life. 'Poetry has lost its old audience,' he said in 1957, two years after the publication of *The Less Deceived*. 'This has been caused by the consequences of a cunning merger between poet, literary critic and academic critic (three classes now notoriously indistinguishable).'[1] Over the last twenty-five years, at regular intervals, he has made the same objection: 'the dutiful mob that signs on every September' has been the target of his emphatic scorn, while the unspecialized 'pleasure-seeking audience'[2] has been complimented and courted. Faced with this hostility, critics can only accept that their role is a superfluous or invidious one. His comments on his poetry are clearly designed to embarrass or even exclude them, either by denigrating their methods or by revealing little about his intentions. He has always cultivated his privacy, and declined almost every invitation to read and discuss his work. But it is an unavoidable result of his reticence that the occasions on which it has been breached have acquired a special significance. By appearing only infrequently, his statements have a resonance lacking in those that come from comparatively talkative writers. And for all his antipathy to critics – perhaps, indeed, because of that antipathy – he has been at pains to give them a clear picture of his poetic personality and prejudices.

Larkin's readers, academic and otherwise, have tended to judge him by these rare self-revelations. His main purpose has been to direct attention to the expository, documentary, empirical and rational elements in his poetry. These are qualities evident in work by other members of the Movement – the British literary group with which he was originally identified in the 1950s – and they are also apparent in the earlier poet he has most frequently and candidly praised: Thomas Hardy. As one might expect, this emphasis has been accompanied by an attempt to discredit writers who do not conform to the same pattern: T. S. Eliot, Ezra Pound, and the whole range of modernist artists with whom they were associated. The French symbolist writers of the 1890s, who crucially helped to shape Eliot's poetry and were deeply involved in the development of modernism, have also been abused. Their obscurities and irrationalities, and their subversions of traditional poetic methods, are – on the face of it – entirely at odds with Larkin's own practice. 'Poetry is an affair of sanity, of seeing things as they are,'[3] he has staunchly insisted.

But, in spite of what he would have us believe, Larkin has in fact absorbed and adapted a number of strategies that derive from the modernists in general and the symbolists in particular. There is an important circumstantial explanation for this: Larkin's most formative early influence was W. B. Yeats, whose own poetry owed a great deal to the symbolists – and Yeats's description of their methods helps to explain their appeal to Larkin. In 'The Symbolism of Poetry' (1900), Yeats argued that 'Because an emotion does not exist, or does not become perceptible and active among us, till it has found its expression, in colour or in sound or in form, or in all three of these, and because no two modulations or arrangements of these evoke the same emotion, poets and painters and musicians . . . are continually making and unmaking mankind.'[4] Mere 'metaphors', he insisted, 'are not profound enough'[5] to fulfil this function of arousing emotion. The most revealing aspect of this definition is, paradoxically, its vagueness. Although it seems to suggest that Yeats was drawn to symbolism simply because it offered him a way of creating mood and conveying strong emotion, it also indicates that imprecision itself was important. Yeats's remark implies – and the whole essay confirms this – that to dislocate the precise relationship between a concept and a thing was to transcend the ordinary world and so escape the flow of time. To evoke a series of illogical and obscure connections, in other words, was to create an artifice of eternity. The French symbolist poets went much further than Yeats in pursuit of this goal. Mallarmé spoke for all his associates when he wrote 'To name an object is to do away with three-quarters of the enjoyment of the poem which is derived from the satisfaction of guessing little by little: to suggest it, to evoke it – that is what charms the imagination.'[6] In his own work Mallarmé, like Baudelaire, Rimbaud and Verlaine, habitually avoids distinct circumstances, and cultivates what Yeats called 'those wavering, meditative, organic rhythms which are the embodiment of the imagination'.[7] It is these characteristics, of course, that produce what is sometimes regarded as the reprehensible mystification of symbolist poetry. By encouraging personal associations, disconnected images and irrational intimations rather than plain speech, it withdrew itself from familiar reality and cultivated an esoteric – and often rather precious – privacy.

Larkin's use of symbolism is much less marked than Yeats's – as well as being much less precious and much less obscure – but it derives from the same French sources. As Barbara Everett has pointed out in her essay 'Philip Larkin: After Symbolism', particular symbolist poems are often glancingly recalled in his work. 'Sympathy in White Major', for instance, discordantly parodies Théophile Gautier's 'Symphonie en blanc majeur', 'Arrivals, Departures' echoes Baudelaire's 'Le Port', and 'Toads' calls to mind the Chimaeras in Baudelaire's prose poem 'Chacun sa Chimère'.[8] As will become apparent (in Chapter 4), such debts are seldom unqualified, and are usually apparent only for the matter of a stanza or a few lines. But by way of introduction it is worth emphasizing that, even when the influence of specific symbolist poems is not apparent, their

13

strategies are often recalled by Larkin's own. He repeatedly turns away from his closely observed surroundings, or breaks a strictly rational discourse, by introducing a bizarre and seemingly unrelated element. 'Dockery and Son' gives a miniature but good example: the 'sand-clouds' that appear in the last stanza have no precise connection with the poem's dominant pattern of images – the railway lines, which he watches meeting and parting as he contemplates the meetings and partings that have occurred in his life. The sand-clouds, that is to say, disturb the empirical progression of the poem, and their effect is typical of all such interruptions in Larkin's work. By creating a brief emotional intensity, and a momentary release from immediate surroundings, they fleetingly fulfil the function that Yeats expected of symbolism.

Larkin has frequently denied the existence of such moments in his work. In the Introduction to the 1966 reissue of his first collection, *The North Ship*, he describes how, soon after he had put the book together in 1945, Hardy replaced Yeats as his main influence. He implies that this exchange swiftly and absolutely abolished his symbolist sympathies, and this impression has been confirmed by a number of subsequent remarks. When Ian Hamilton, for instance, asked him 'Do you ever read any foreign poetry?', Larkin replied '*Foreign* poetry? *No!*'[9] But a notebook covering the period 1944–50, and the evidence of such poems as those mentioned above, shows his change of allegiance to have been far more protracted and difficult than he has suggested. To realize this is not simply to highlight an overlooked aspect of Larkin's poetry, but to challenge the popular idea that he has not developed as a writer. The almost purely symbolist moments of *The Less Deceived* (1955) – 'Coming', for instance, or 'Dry Point', or 'Going' – are nowhere to be found in *The Whitsun Weddings* (1964), which of all his books is the one owing most to Hardy's example. But the later volume *High Windows* (1974) makes it impossible to agree with the definition that Larkin gave of himself in 1966 as a 'patient sleeping soundly' (*NS*, p. 10) after his Celtic fever had abated. 'High Windows' itself, 'Sympathy in White Major', 'Livings' Part II, 'Solar' and 'Money' – to name only a few of the poems in this volume – expose and dramatize differences between the empirical mode associated with Hardy and the symbolist mode associated with Yeats. Larkin did not simply swap Yeats for Hardy early in his career. The aspect of his personality to which Yeats originally appealed has been radically modified in his maturity – but it has endured, and much of his best work takes the form of a dialectic between the attitudes and qualities of his two mentors.

*

Larkin's involvement with Yeats and Hardy represents, in miniature, that struggle between two different literary traditions which has dominated English poetry for the last sixty-odd years. For modern poets, the 'tradition' has been an anxious affair: in 1919 it was still possible for Eliot to claim, in his influential essay 'Tradition and the Individual Talent', that

> In English writing we seldom speak of tradition, though we occasionally apply its name in deploring its absence. We cannot refer to 'the tradition' or to 'a tradition'; at most, we employ the adjective in saying that the poetry of So-and-so is 'traditional' or even 'too traditional'.[10]

At the same time Eliot emphasized that traditions were not inert qualities but had to be struggled for with great labour, and that in periods of major innovation they were considerably remade. Eliot belonged to a fundamental phase of such remaking, the era of Pound's 'Make It New'; and it was part of the achievement of both to challenge the received literary orthodoxy. Where Eliot's and Pound's English contemporaries, the Georgians, made only slight changes to the nineteenth-century legacy, and were conventionally formal, pastoral, accessible and provincial, Eliot – along with other modernists in the Anglo-American line – was unconventional, urban, difficult, cosmopolitan, sympathetic to symbolism and, above all, determined to reconceive the relationship between modern poetry and the poetry of the past.

15

In the event, the modernist intervention succeeded; during the years after the First World War the aesthetics and effects of the internationalist spirit of modernism almost completely obliterated, in serious poetry, the native English tradition. A new experimentalism, derived from symbolism, from Pound's Anglo-American movement of Imagism, and from a sense of the fragmentation of past poetic culture, dominated. Hardy survived as a special case, and so – for a much smaller audience – did Edward Thomas. But the Georgians, with some justice, were isolated, and ridiculed as the purveyors of nostalgia for a world, and the poetic forms of a world, that no longer existed. In the 1930s, however, the balance began to readjust. W. H. Auden's early poems assented to modernism's influence, and Eliot's and Yeats's power: they inherited the sense of modern cultural crisis. But they also described, as the poetry of Eliot, Pound and Yeats did not, a recognizably English landscape in an unmistakably English tone of voice. Auden's formality, for instance, and his occasional use of the English alliterative line, represented a calculated blow to the 'foreignness' of the modernist poets, even though he expressed a strikingly contemporary sensibility.

By this time, then, the two traditions – native English and modernist – were clearly established; sometimes they merged, but often they attracted mutually hostile advocates. And those battle-lines have remained through subsequent generations of British poetry, generally separating it from the development of modernism that took place in the United States. So, in his influential anthology *The New Poetry* (1962), collected after a new generation of post-war British poets had begun to take shape, A. Alvarez attacked Auden's efforts to reconstruct the tradition as the first of a series of 'negative feed-backs'.[11] Alvarez saw this continuing in the work of Dylan Thomas and then acquiring a kind of unhealthy strength in the work of the newer poets of the Movement, which emerged in the 1950s. He argued, in a debate that closely paralleled similar contemporary discussions about the direction of the novel, that the Movement poets paid a price for their traditionally English stance – in an exaggerated provincialism, insularity, dullness, and a blunt refusal to learn from the experiments, the imaginative excitements and the post-symbolist aesthetics associated with Eliot and modernism. Indeed, around the time *The New Poetry* came out, the argument between the proponents of modernism and what became known as 'the English line' had degenerated – as these things usually do – into bickering and squabbling, and versions of it still continue. One of the most damaging consequences was to distort the actual character and achievement of a number of poets caught in the quarrel. Larkin was undoubtedly the most distinguished member of the Movement (other names associated with it include Thom Gunn, Donald Davie, John Wain, D. J. Enright and Kingsley Amis), and he attracted most of the fire. On many occasions he was made to seem (and often made himself seem) a pillar of the provincial establishment, prissily genteel and creatively timid – a view that obscured his real achievement. And when commentators attempted to rescue him from such criticism and abuse they often chose to emphasize his supposed narrowness in order to make a virtue of it. Donald Davie, for example, in his study *Thomas Hardy and British Poetry*, hitched Larkin firmly to Hardy and asked: 'Are not Hardy and his successors right in severely curtailing for themselves the liberties that other poets continued to take? Does not the example of the Hardyesque poets make some of the other [modernist] poets look childishly irresponsible?'[12]

In fact, Larkin has done far more to relate the modernists to 'the English line' than his friends or enemies have been prepared to admit, or than his own remarks suggest. But, since the rest of this book seeks to establish his largely ignored adaptation of symbolist – and therefore by association modernist – strategies, it is important to stress at the start that his sense of the English tradition is extraordinarily acute. When he rejected Yeats in favour of Hardy, he did so at least partly because he felt that Yeats shared – in an admittedly less extreme form – the same alien subversiveness and 'irresponsibility' (*AWJ*, p. 11) that he criticized in Eliot and Pound. The modernists' charac-

17

teristic preoccupation with technique was the main cause for complaint:

> The poetry I've enjoyed has been the kind of poetry you'd associate with me, Hardy pre-eminently, Wilfred Owen, Auden, Christina Rossetti, William Barnes; on the whole, people to whom technique seems to matter less than content, people who accept the forms they have inherited but use them to express their own content.[13]

As he makes abundantly plain in his Introduction to *All What Jazz: A Record Diary* (1970), it is not simply experimentation he deplores but the fact that artists who cultivate a relationship with their material rather than with their audience will become prey to 'the two principal themes of modernism, mystification and outrage':

> This is my essential criticism of modernism, whether perpetrated by Parker, Pound or Picasso: it helps us neither to enjoy nor endure. It will divert as long as we are prepared to be mystified or outraged, but maintains its hold only by being more mystifying and more outrageous: it has no lasting power. Hence the compulsion of every modernist to wade deeper and deeper into violence and obscenity. (*AWJ*, p. 17)

This is a direct challenge to Eliot's insistence that 'Poets in our civilization, as it exists at present, must be difficult' – and, although Larkin's own poems have been called complex on a number of occasions, he has always maintained a distinction between 'what is unnecessarily obscure and what is properly hard to understand because the complexity of the subject demands difficulty'.[14]

Critics, given half a chance, confound this differentiation. 'Modern criticism thrives on the difficult', Larkin has claimed, '– either in explaining the difficult or in explaining that what seemed straightforward is in fact difficult'.[15] In developing this line of argument, he has isolated another modernist trait for condemnation. *The Waste Land* and *Ulysses*, for example, contain copious references to, and quotation from, other texts and thereby make themselves into complex and many-layered literary palimpsests. In Larkin's view this has encouraged 'a view of poetry which is almost mechanistic, that every poem must include all previous poems, in the same way that a Ford Zephyr has somewhere in it a Ford T Model'[16] – and in *Poets of the 1950s* he made the same point with infamous clarity: 'As a guiding principle I believe that every poem must be its own sole freshly-created universe, and therefore have no belief in "tradition" or a common myth-kitty, which last I find unpleasantly like the talk of literary under-strappers letting you see they know the right people.'[17]

Larkin's rejection of the 'evolutionary view'[18] of poetry espoused by the modernists has left him in a paradoxical position. While professing to have 'no belief in "tradition"', he has nevertheless been at pains to associate himself with the specifically English line. As it appears in his work, this feeds into him from – among others – Wordsworth, Tennyson, Hardy, Edward Thomas, A. E. Housman and Auden. It also nourishes, of course, a large number of other recent poets who have not been directly associated with the Movement – notably the contemporary poet he particularly admires, John Betjeman. Larkin has a variety of concerns in common with these earlier English poets. For one thing, they all use a moderate tone of voice and accessible language – the 'language such as men do use'. For another, they are all centrally concerned with the relationship between themselves and their towns or landscapes, and habitually express a sense of communion with their surroundings in exalted or even semi-mystical terms. They are all, that is to say, intensely patriotic poets, though not all of them need the presence of war to crystallize their feelings, and none of them shapes their emotional and intellectual involvement with England in any other than the most unjingoistic language.

But Larkin has never allowed a consciously English attitude and formal practice to become inhibitingly *self*-conscious. Although he has flatly rejected modernism in theory, in practice – as will become clear – he is a remarkably inclusive writer. It is this flexibility, and his capacity to create a recognizable and democratic vision of contemporary society, that has made him such a potent force in modern English poetry. It is difficult to think of a living English writer who has exercised a stronger influence on his own and the next generation. At one time it seemed as if Ted Hughes might share the honours, but the very particular accent and emphasis of Hughes's poetry has inhibited its effect. Seamus Heaney, who might be regarded as the most distinguished poet to have emerged in the last twenty years, undoubtedly owes debts to both of them: the barbarous pastoralism of his early poems is obviously reminiscent of Hughes, but it is contained by a formal orthodoxy and explicatory tone that distinctly recalls Larkin. In the work of several other poets who came to prominence during the 1960s – Anthony Thwaite, for instance, or Alan Brownjohn – Larkin's subjects and cadences are even more noticeable.

Considerations such as these make it essential to include an appreciation of Larkin's work in any discussion of recent writing; he has done more than any other living poet to solve the crisis that beset British poetry after the modernists had entered its bloodstream. He has not only made evident what Edna Longley has called 'a significant coincidence and continuity of effort'[19] with the interrupted English tradition; he has revitalized existing strengths by introducing them to elements of the poetic revolution by which they were challenged.

It is now almost thirty years since Larkin's first mature book of poems was published, and it would be surprising if more recent poets had not adapted his example. Largely because of his success in welding together two previously antagonistic traditions, several younger poets have felt able to write without taking aggressively pro- or anti-modernist attitudes. Much recent English poetry is characterized by such a synthesis of modernism and the 'English line'. To take just one example, a number of young poets are interested in writing narratives: Paul Muldoon, for instance, in 'Immram', or James Fenton in 'A German Requiem', have managed to combine familiar and time-honoured techniques of storytelling with a degree of literary self-awareness and self-irony which the modernists made part of their stock-in-trade. This kind of synthesis is something that Larkin has done an enormous amount to facilitate. His achievement is a major one – but it is hard to imagine a more modest and, in some respects, a more reluctant pioneer.

2

THE BACKGROUND

Larkin has always been at pains to make his life seem at best unremarkable and at worst dull. On one occasion he claimed that his biography could begin when he was twenty-one and omit nothing of importance;[20] on another he described his childhood as a 'forgotten boredom' (*LD*, p. 17); and he has persistently stressed the lack of spectacular events in his experience as an adult. One of his best-known poems, 'I Remember, I Remember', recalls his youth as a time of dire nullity, and implies that in later years he has found that 'Nothing, like something, happens anywhere' too. Why has he mocked or suppressed details of his past so ruthlessly? One reason is an understandable desire to preserve what is his own and nobody else's business. But there are more strictly literary considerations as well. By obliterating his childhood, Larkin has asserted his independence as an adult – in 'I Remember, I Remember' he shakes free from his former self and at the same time denies popular Romantic and Lawrentian notions of childhood. The poem is an expression of personal and literary autonomy, even though it describes its speaker as a prisoner of disappointment.

By destroying or forgetting the excitements of his youth, Larkin has made it conform to the picture of his mature life as a 'simple ordinary man in an unromantic modern world'.[21] But, even supposing this version of himself were broadly true, it would clearly be absurd to conclude that retiring orthodoxy implied an absence of emotional and intellectual intensity. In fact, if a remark made about Vernon Watkins is anything to go by, Larkin's decision to live as he has done is a deliberate attempt to perfect the work, rather than pack the life with incident. Watkins, he said, 'showed me how the conventional life was compatible with total devotion to poetry. I can't believe that one needs violent experience to write something especially revealing. You don't need a palate for pepper.'[22]

Larkin's 'conventional life' began in Coventry on 9 August 1922 – the year his father was made City Treasurer. It was, he has said, 'a solid background in which everybody worked. No question about it. It was immoral not to work.'[23] In 1930 he was sent to one of the town's two direct-grant schools, King Henry VIII School, where if his own report is to be believed he was 'very stupid until he could concentrate on English'.[24] Stupidity notwithstanding, he spent much of his time playing and devising complex board games and reading 'at the rate of a book a day, even despite the tiresome interruptions of morning and afternoon school'.[25] For the most part, this was a matter of devouring whatever came his way – his parents owned a considerable number of books, and they were not in the least censorious. Years later Larkin said: 'Not until I was much older did I realise that most boys of my class were brought up to regard Galsworthy and Chesterton as the apex of modern literature, and to think Somerset Maugham a bit "hot". I was therefore lucky.'[26] At the same time as his enthusiasm for reading developed, so did his interest in writing. He contributed (largely humorous) prose pieces and poems to the school magazine, and worked with a fluency that was to desert him in later life. He recalls producing 'now verse, which I sewed up into little books, now prose, a thousand words a night after homework'.[27]

Perhaps it is such evidence of studiousness that has helped to create the impression of Larkin, by the time he went to read English at St John's College, Oxford, in 1940, as inflexibly introverted. Although certainly withdrawn – his shyness was intensified by a bad stammer – he had a marked streak of ebullience. His friend Bruce Montgomery described him as a 'massive, affable, pipe-smoking undergraduate'.[28] He was, for

23

instance, a member of the university jazz club (he had wanted to be a drummer when still at school), and also of the English Society. Eventually he became treasurer of the latter, and helped to organize a number of visits from celebrated writers, including Dylan Thomas, George Orwell and Vernon Watkins. His own reputation as a writer was, within the university, quickly established. Although he had gone up a year early because he expected to have to join the forces, he had already published a poem, 'Ultimatum', in *The Listener*. His literary ambitions were matched and stimulated by other members of his college and the university. As it was wartime, the turnover of undergraduates was more erratic than usual, and the chances of forming longstanding relationships diminished. But when, after four terms, Larkin failed his army medical and was therefore allowed to remain at Oxford the full nine terms, he was able to realize a degree of stability for himself, while acquaintances quickly came and went. His friends included Alan Ross, John Wain, Diana Gollancz, Edward du Cann and, pre-eminently, Kingsley Amis. Amis, more than anyone else, helped Larkin to clarify his literary aims and ambitions – largely by urging him to reject youthful romantic pretensions in favour of a more robust, ironical attitude to experience.

Amis's influence was, in turn, corroborated by the prejudices of their tutor, the Anglo-Saxon scholar Gavin Bone. Several of Larkin's schoolboy poems had borrowed extensively from Eliot, but Bone's dislike of the modernists was absolute. His two pupils' burgeoning antipathy to avant-garde obscurities was encouraged by his example. The social and political atmosphere of Oxford itself, too, encouraged a pragmatic approach to life, as to literature. In the Introduction to the 1964 reissue of *Jill*, Larkin remembered that 'A lack of *douceur* was balanced by a lack of *bêtises*, whether of college ceremonial or undergraduate extravagance. . . . At an age when self-importance would have been normal, events cut us ruthlessly down to size' (*J*, p. 12).

Larkin has recalled his academic career at Oxford with the same self-mocking modesty that he has used to describe his schooldays. 'The highest academic compliment I received was "Mr Larkin can see a point, if it is explained to him"' (*J*, p. 14). This clearly misrepresents his abilities: although he burnt his notes in December 1941, in anticipation of being called up, he still managed to get a first-class degree when he sat the exams in the summer of 1943. But he had no firm ideas about a career – partly, no doubt, for the same reason that the heroes of his two novels feel disorientated and dissatisfied: the war. John Kemp says that because of the war his life had 'no continuity' (*J*, p. 144), and Robin Fennel admits that it has 'Broken the sequence' (*GW*, p. 246) of his experience. Larkin applied for a number of jobs 'almost at random'[29] and late in 1943 was appointed librarian at the public library in Wellington, Shropshire, where he stayed for the next three years. 'That', he says, 'seems to have determined the course of my life.'[30] Although he felt isolated at Wellington, and lived in cold and uncongenial digs, the town was at least peaceful and undistracting. Every night he would work in his lodgings from 9 o'clock until midnight – and produced a large amount of poetry and prose. In 1945 several of his poems were included in *Poetry from Oxford in Wartime*, an anthology edited by William Bell and published by the Fortune Press. This was run by R. A. Caton (later stigmatized by Amis in several novels as an incompetent crook – L. S. Caton), who admired Larkin's work and invited him to submit some more with a view to publishing a full-length collection. Larkin sent thirty, and the result was *The North Ship*, which also appeared in 1945. The following year the Fortune Press published Larkin's first novel, *Jill* (which was dedicated to Amis), but his relationship with Caton developed no further. Shortly after the book appeared, Larkin moved to take up a job in the library of what was then University College, Leicester, and his next novel, *A Girl in Winter* (1947), was published by Faber & Faber.

No sooner was *A Girl in Winter* finished than Larkin began work on a third novel, which came to nothing more than a vain 'long dreary attempt'.[31] With regard to his writing, at least, his time at Leicester seems to have been disappointing. His notebook for the period contains many unpublished poems and fragments in the style of *The North Ship*, and one act of an unsuccessful verse play, 'Night in the Plague'. In 1948 he attempted to publish a second collection of twenty-five poems, which he intended to call 'In the Grip of Light'. It was turned down by Faber & Faber, John Lane, Dent, Macmillan, Methuen and John Lehmann.[32] In 1950, however, he was appointed sub-librarian at Queen's University, Belfast, and the move accelerated the development of his talent. Abandoning the third novel seems to have allowed him to concentrate what he obviously regarded as prose virtues in his poems, and Belfast's geographical remoteness from his former existence gave him the chance to assess himself and his past more objectively. The year after arriving in Northern Ireland, he collected twenty of his best early poems, had them privately printed as a pamphlet and sent copies to a number of leading literary figures. But their merits went unappreciated: most of the addressees failed to reply, no doubt partly because Larkin had 'understamped the envelopes at a time when the postal charges had just been increased'.[33]

Thirteen of Larkin's *XX Poems* eventually appeared in *The Less Deceived* – 'Wedding Wind', 'Next, Please', 'Deceptions', 'Latest Face', 'Spring', 'Dry Point', 'Coming', 'No Road', 'If, My Darling', 'Wires', 'Wants', 'Going' and 'At Grass'. He had already discovered the distinctive features of his poetic personality, and for the next few years continued to enlarge its resources. 'I wrote the bulk of *The Less Deceived* in Belfast', he said later, 'under no particular influence except Kingsley's. I'd visions of showing him things he would laugh at. It's a formidable experience to be laughed at by Kingsley.'[34] In 1953 a selection of his work was published by G. S. Fraser and Ian Fletcher in their anthology *Springtime*, in 1954 five of his poems appeared in a Fantasy Press pamphlet, and later the same year he completed *The Less Deceived* itself. The typescript was considered, and rejected, by Liam Miller at the Dolmen Press before George Hartley, who ran the Marvell Press at Hessle, near Hull, asked to see it. Larkin sent it under the title *Various Poems*. It was accepted and published in 1955 (the title was changed at Hartley's insistence) and immediately attracted extremely favourable attention. The initial subscription issue of 300 copies was quickly exhausted, and the book was reprinted three times in the first nine months after its publication. Larkin's reputation has climbed steeply ever since, and in the early days its spread was quickened by his association with the Movement. Most of the young writers in this group, including Larkin himself, had had some of their work included in D. J. Enright's anthology *Poets of the 1950s*, which was published in Tokyo in 1950, and in 1956 Robert Conquest's anthology *New Lines* brought them to a wider audience at home.

Within weeks of Hartley's accepting *The Less Deceived*, Larkin had, by coincidence, become his near neighbour. He had applied for and been offered the post of librarian at the University of Hull library (now the Brynmor Jones Library) – a position he still holds. To start with, he has often said, the job was 'a nice little Shetland pony', but it has since grown into 'a frightful Grand National winner'.[35] In 1982, after government cuts to the universities, his job was to cater for the library needs of 5,600 students, to supervise the 96 members of the library staff, and to arbitrate between departments in spending an annual budget of £37,300 on books and periodicals.[36] Hull itself has given him the same mixture of security and isolation he looked for elsewhere – 'Any really thorough-going egoist', he has claimed, 'does not take much account of his surroundings, as long as they do not actively bother him';[37] and his modesty and habits of seclusion have remained unwavering during his time there. In fact, since the beginning of Larkin's celebrity coincided with his move to Hull, the public's impression of him is derived almost exclusively from the style in which he has lived there. And although never very eventful – at least to outward appearances – the tenor of his way has become increasingly even since his arrival in the city. In addition to publishing a selection of his jazz reviews, *All What Jazz* (1970), and editing *The Oxford Book of Twentieth-Century English*

27

Verse (1973), he has produced only two more collections of poetry: *The Whitsun Weddings* (1964) and *High Windows* (1974). The respect and honour that these have brought him – the Queen's Gold Medal for Poetry in 1965, honorary doctorates from the Universities of Belfast, Leicester, Warwick, St Andrews and Sussex, and six months as a Visiting Fellow of All Souls College, Oxford – have been accompanied by publicity from which he has assiduously defended himself. His occasional reviews are littered with remarks repudiating the supposed pleasures of community life in general and the family in particular. His dislike of travel and holidays springs from a similar concern for privacy, stability and self-reliance: 'As I get older I grow increasingly impatient of holidays : they seem a wholly feminine conception, based on an impotent dislike of everyday life and a romantic notion that it will all be better at Frinton or Venice.'[38] As a young man, this determination to shed all traces of illusion was the outward and social sign of his inward and literary intentions: it was the expression of his attempts to destroy his original Yeatsian mask. Now, in his maturity, the attitudes have themselves become a mask – one that is intensely self-knowing, as well as protective.

*

Having sketched the outline of Larkin's 'private' life it is worth giving the background to his literary one.

Larkin's literary beliefs are commonly supposed not to have changed much in the last forty-odd years. The relatively recent Oxford anthology exemplifies attitudes that seem substantially the same as those he evolved in the late 1940s. Taken with the Introduction to *All What Jazz*, the book amounts to a statement of poetic intent delivered towards the end of his writing life rather than at the beginning. The anonymous reviewer in *The Times Literary Supplement* summarized its main points: 'other than an hostility to Modernism, either official (i.e. Franco-American) or homegrown, his selection shows two notable leanings or quirks of taste. He dislikes obscurity in poetry, and he is romantically patriotic.'[39] These comments direct our attention towards a crucial factor in Larkin's evolution as a poet – and it is one that he has commented upon himself. When the anthology was published in 1973, Larkin told Anthony Thwaite:

> I had in my mind a notion that there might have been what I'll call, for want of a better phrase, an English tradition coming from the nineteenth century with people like Hardy, which was interrupted partly by the Great War, when many English poets were killed off, and partly by the really tremendous impact of Yeats, whom I think of as Celtic, and Eliot, whom I think of as American.[40]

In other words, the *Oxford Book of Twentieth-Century English Verse* amounts to a kind of literary patriotism – an attempt to celebrate the ideal he began to define for himself at Oxford during the war. Several of his contemporaries responded to the social and political climate of their youth in the same way: like his, their literary ambitions were crucially shaped by threats from abroad and deprivations and disillusionment at home.

Many of Larkin's most distinguished contemporary writers met at Oxford as undergraduates, and many were originally published by the Fantasy Press. But their first close association in public was stage-managed – and their name given – by an anonymous journalist[41] in the *Spectator* on 1 October 1954:

> The Movement, as well as being anti-phoney, is anti-wet; sceptical, robust, ironic, prepared to be as comfortable as possible in a wicked, commercial, threatened world which doesn't look, anyway, as if it's going to be changed much by a couple of handfuls of young English writers.[42]

This article appeared the year before D. J. Enright's *Poets of the 1950s*, and two years before an anthology which included almost exactly the same contributors[43] and was to give the Movement its clearest definition: Robert Conquest's *New Lines*. The writers included were Larkin, Donald Davie, Robert Conquest, Thom Gunn, John Hollander, Kingsley

Amis, John Wain, D. J. Enright and Elizabeth Jennings, and they were introduced with jaunty defiance:

> If one had briefly to distinguish this poetry of the fifties from its predecessors, I believe the most important general point would be that it submits to no great systems of theoretical constructs nor agglomerations of unconscious commands. It is free from both mystical and logical compulsions and – like modern philosophy – is empirical in its attitude to all that comes. This reverence for the real person or event is, indeed, a part of the general intellectual ambience . . . of our time.[44]

Conquest's approval of the poets' 'refusal to abandon a rational structure and comprehensible language' was a specific challenge to modernism, though once that had been given the Introduction crumbled into uncertainty: 'What they do have in common is perhaps, at its lowest, little more than a negative determination to avoid bad principles.'[45] But, for all its lack of positive characterization, this was the first and one of the most striking attempts to sell Larkin as he has subsequently been received, and to ignore elements in his poems which depart from the Movement's orthodoxy.

It is, however, undeniably true that one characteristic tone of Larkin's work closely answers Conquest's description of the archetypal Movement poem. In 'Church Going', for instance, or 'Lines on a Young Lady's Photograph Album', or 'Toads', he creates an ironic and self-critical persona – and it is this that the war, and its attendant social conditions, did so much to foster. As well as stimulating a resilient and protective love for England and its traditions, the war significantly narrowed the country's social divisions and cleared the way for interest and pride in what had previously been condemned as 'ordinary'. The levelling democratizing process which has gathered strength throughout this century, and which was accelerated between 1939 and 1945 just as it was between 1914 and 1918, released Larkin's scrupulously unremarkable figures for duty in poems as speakers rather than merely as suffering subjects.

Donald Davie, in his critical book *Purity of Diction in*

English Verse, expressed his ambitions in terms that speak for the Movement as a whole, and Larkin, Amis and Conquest in particular: 'I should like to think that this study might help some practising poet to a poetry of urbane and momentous statement.'[46] The same principles applied to the group's typical choice of subject. Recherché themes were as frowned-upon as much as rarefied poetic language, and any idea that artists should exist in precious isolation was scorned. Amis was especially outspoken: 'nobody wants any more poems on the grander themes for a few years, but at the same time nobody wants more poems about philosophers or paintings or novelists or art galleries or mythology or foreign cities or other poems.'[47] In all such statements the poet is removed from a garret or ivory tower and put firmly on the street; it was, in Alvarez's words, 'an attempt to show that the poet is not a strange creature inspired; on the contrary, he is just like the man next door – in fact, he probably *is* the man next door.'[48]

There are, however, a number of revealing paradoxes in the Movement's democratic manner. At the same time as the Movement poets felt free to scorn class barriers, they remained intensely class-conscious. Blake Morrison, in his history of the Movement, points out how Larkin, in particular, is careful to create a recognizable no-nonsense middle-class tone in his work – partly by adopting the terms of reasonable argument typified by a poem like 'Reasons for Attendance', and partly by a judicious sprinkling of throwaway phrases: 'I'm afraid', 'it seems', 'of course', 'Too subtle that, too decent too. Oh hell.' These are ways of suggesting a mind following a line of thought, and often of realizing something plausibly 'true' for the first time, and they are also a means of registering the speakers' social position. Their calculating modesty disallows any chance of bardic pretensions, and asserts itself as uncompromisingly middlebrow, as in 'Self's the Man':

> To compare his life and mine
> Makes me feel a swine:
> Oh, no one can deny
> That Arnold is less selfish than I.

31

But wait, not so fast:
Is there such a contrast?
He was out for his own ends
Not just pleasing his friends;

And if it was such a mistake
He still did it for his own sake,
Playing his own game.
So he and I are the same,

Only I'm a better hand
At knowing what I can stand
Without them sending a van –
Or I suppose I can. (*WW*, pp. 24–5)

In spite of their efforts to strip poems and poets of any isolating mystery, their tone of voice cannot help creating its own clannishness. Morrison has noticed that in just over a third of Larkin's mature work the speaker speaks as 'we' rather than 'I', and that the word is less often used familiarly 'than in the sense of "our generation" or even "the group of us"'.[49] This impression of special pleading counteracts the emphasis of their typically humdrum language and terms of reference – as does the polished formality of their work and its unshakeable (sometimes rather superiorly knowing) lack of illusion. At one time they were even referred to as 'the new University wits'[50] – and with some justification, as Amis has pointed out: 'All the people writing [Movement poetry] were dons, and all the people reviewing it were dons, and all the people who were reading it were dons, and so on. So you've got a kind of donnish poetry.'[51] These considerations make it impossible not to charge the Movement poets with something that – as upholders of the English tradition – they sought to stamp out: élitism. This, they felt, was one of the modernists' besetting sins: Eliot's complexity had taken poetry away from a general public and put it in the classroom. Yet the Movement's own tone, class assumptions and specifically English emphasis implied a kind of exclusivity.

This internal contradiction is paralleled by another significant discrepancy between Larkin's poetry and his expressed principles. When he stated that during the late 1940s Hardy had replaced Yeats as his main influence, he summarized the Movement's most important and character-forming allegiances. Yeats, as a foreign, bardic, imperious modernist, embodied most of the qualities deplored by the Movement writers; Hardy, as an English, plain-speaking, pragmatic traditionalist, represented most of the virtues they admired. Yet despite these views the influence of Yeats has continued to shape even Larkin's most recent work.

Larkin was first introduced to Yeats's poems by Vernon Watkins at a meeting of the Oxford English Club in 1943, and their appeal was instant:

> I spent the next three years trying to write like Yeats, not because I liked his personality or understood his ideas but out of infatuation with his music. . . . In fairness to myself it must be admitted that it is a particularly potent music, pervasive as garlic, and has ruined many a better talent. (NS, p. 9)

Shortly after Watkins's talk, Larkin left Oxford for Wellington and began reading Yeats for himself, using a copy stolen from a local girls' school. It was the 1933 edition of the *Collected Poems* – a fact that was vital in determining the verbal structures and cadences he imitated. Instead of the 'harsher last poems' (NS, p. 10), he based his work on *fin de siècle* models and symbolist strategies. The results, some of which eventually formed *The North Ship*, are almost all languorously drooping in their rhythms and uninventively romantic in their references. They frequently borrow direct from Yeats, and general resemblances abound. Their mood is invariably gloomy without justification, their time of day dawn or dusk, their weather cold, rainy and windy, and their symbolic details monotonous: water, stars, ice, ships, candles, dreams, hands and beds occur with extraordinary frequency and no distinguishing features:

To write one song, I said,
As sad as the sad wind
That walks around my bed,
Having one simple fall
As a candle-flame swells, and is thinned,
As a curtain stirs by the wall
– For this I must visit the dead.
Headstone and wet cross,
Paths where the mourners tread,
A solitary bird,
These call up the shade of loss,
Shape word to word. (*NS*, p. 29)

There is nothing of Yeats's vitality in these poems but, rather, a sentimental version of Yeats's preoccupation with love, sexual *tristesse* and death – all of which survive, toughened, in his mature poems. The impression they leave, as Alan Brownjohn admits,

> is that of a poet struggling sensitively – with unambitious technical care rather than verbal energy or imaginative stamina – to pit some private experience of exhilaration and release, or some recurrent images of purity and vitality in nature, against the dullness of ordinary existence and the prevailing sense of death; so the later Larkin *is* here, though writ very small.[52]

As it appears in *The North Ship*, Yeats's initial effect on Larkin seems to have been almost completely deleterious. It is hardly surprising, therefore, that Larkin should seek to dissociate his mature style from its origins. In the reissue of *The North Ship* he included a poem, 'Waiting for breakfast', written 'a year or so' (*NS*, p. 10) after the book had been completed (actually on 15 December 1947). The poem is a monologue, spoken by a man in a hotel room while the woman with whom he has spent the night is making herself ready for breakfast. Its tones of voice clearly illustrate the early stages of his revulsion from Yeats. 'It wasn't', he modestly told Ian Hamilton, 'any conscious reaction. It's just that when you start writing your own stuff other people's manners won't really do for it.'[53] But in fact another poet's 'manners' are precisely what he adopted. 'I looked to Hardy', he admitted, 'rather than Yeats as my ideal, and eventually a more rational approach, less hysterical and emphatic, asserted itself'.[54] In 'Waiting for breakfast' the characteristics of both his mentors are strongly evident: the poem provides an important early example of the tension between distinct qualities which appears in much of his later work. To take the Hardyesque element first. For one thing, Larkin echoes Hardy's poem 'At the Word "Farewell"': the lines 'Turning, I kissed her, / Easily for sheer joy tipping the balance to love' recall Hardy's 'Even then the scale might have turned / Against love by a feather, / – But crimson one cheek of hers burned / When we came in together.' For another, the poem's replacement of *fin de siècle* tactics with energetic rhythms and familiar details has benefited in more general terms from Hardy's emotional fidelity to facts. 'When I came to Hardy', Larkin has said, 'it was with the sense of relief that I didn't have to try and jack myself up to a concept of poetry that lay outside my own life – this is perhaps what I felt Yeats was trying to make me do. . . . Hardy taught me to feel rather than to write.'[55] But Hardy's way of feeling involved a way of looking – clear-sightedly, and without illusions:

> Waiting for breakfast, while she brushed her hair,
> I looked down at the empty hotel yard
> Once meant for coaches. Cobblestones were wet,
> But sent no light back to the loaded sky,
> Sunk as it was with mist down to the roofs. (*NS*, p. 48)

But, while showing that Larkin was 'beginning to see himself in the context of the real world',[56] 'Waiting for breakfast' also indicates – admittedly clumsily – one important way in which Yeats's influence was to linger. In the first stanza an empirical approach is clearly dominant. In the second, it is momentarily

35

set aside as the speaker realizes his experience in the hotel amounts to more than simply 'Featureless morning, featureless night.' It restores, in fact, a long-vanished feeling of excited happiness. His original methods reassert themselves in a more controlled form:

> the lights burnt on,
> Pin-points of undisturbed excitement; beyond the glass
> The colourless vial of day painlessly spilled
> My world back after a year, my lost lost world
> Like a cropping deer strayed near my path again,
> Bewaring the mind's least clutch. (*NS*, p. 48)

The repetition of 'lost' here reintroduces the rhetorical tone he had repudiated, and the simile of the deer recalls the deployment of symbols in *The North Ship*. In 'Waiting for breakfast' it is restrained, rather than being allowed free rein, and, in spite of its being awkwardly introduced, its very incongruity anticipates a strategy he uses in much later poems like 'Money' and 'High Windows'. The final stanzas of these poems abandon their low-key tone of voice for a rhetorical flourish – and so does 'Waiting for breakfast' itself. As Larkin confronts the possibility of having to choose between a fulfilled social life ('her') and commitment to the Muse ('you'), he rephrases Yeats's remark that writers must choose between perfection of the life and perfection of the work. It was a strikingly suitable poem for Larkin to resurrect and place at the beginning of his mature career:

> But, tender visiting,
> Fallow as a deer or an unforced field,
> How would you have me? Towards your grace
> My promises meet and lock and race like rivers,
> But only when you choose. Are you jealous of her?
> Will you refuse to come till I have sent
> Her terribly away, importantly live
> Part invalid, part baby, and part saint? (*NS*, p. 48)

Larkin has always implied that the qualities he associated

with Yeats, and those associated with Hardy, were mutually exclusive. Abandoning Yeats meant, he has suggested, leaving for ever a world in which it is possible to transcend ordinariness and suffering by the transfiguring dislocations of art, and entering instead a world of historical contingency and attention to particulars, in which to endure suffering is to achieve spiritual wisdom. Yet much of Larkin's best and most characteristic work reconciles these two worlds, and profits by Yeats's example. Several of his formal characteristics obviously derive from Yeats. The model for 'the big matched stanzas' of poems like 'Church Going', 'The Whitsun Weddings', 'The Building', 'Show Saturday' and 'The Old Fools' is what Clive James has called 'the rhetorical majesty'[57] of Yeats's recurrent eight-line stanza – even though the poems' tone and language is reminiscent of Hardy. The commodious flexibility of the form is well summarized by a remark Larkin made to Anthony Thwaite: '[I] would like to write a poem with such elaborate stanzas that one could wander round in them as in the aisles and side-chapels of some great cathedral.'[58] The grandeur that such verse forms encourage is distinctly at odds with Davie's conception of an English poetry of modest ambitions – and so is the rhetorical sweep Larkin allows himself within individual lines and phrases. The conclusion of 'Waiting for breakfast' ('Part invalid, part baby, and part saint'), with its resonant questions, anticipates the rising interrogations of several later poems – 'Wedding Wind', for instance, or 'The Old Fools'.

Similarly, in 'Waiting for breakfast' Larkin collides two different kinds of language: homely monosyllables and polysyllabic adjectival clauses ('the lights burnt on, / Pin-points of undisturbed excitement'). In the process he illustrates a typical strength of his later work. It is not that he replaces one kind of language with another after finishing *The North Ship*, but that he continually juxtaposes the two, and creates a dialogue between aspiring, elevated cadences on the one hand, and all the 'niggling army of modifiers and qualifiers'[59] on the other. 'Vers de Société' is a relatively recent and unmistakable instance:

> *My wife and I have asked a crowd of craps*
> *To come and waste their time and ours: perhaps*
> *You'd care to join us?* In a pig's arse, friend.
> Day comes to an end.
> The gas fire breathes, the trees are darkly swayed.
> And so *Dear Warlock-Williams: I'm afraid* –
>
> (*HW*, p. 35)

Larkin's obscenities are not simple 'manly nudging',[60] as Anthony Thwaite has called them, but a contemporary and brutal version of the diction licensed by the Movement's rather chummy democratic programme. And in 'Vers de Société' they are shockingly juxtaposed with the suggestion of tranquil release (breathing fire, and swaying trees). The poem is a paradigm of Larkin's method: in spite of what he has said, it is clear that, while he inclines temperamentally to the ideal represented by the English line, the Hardyesque languages of isolation and sadness are constantly negotiating in his poems with the Yeatsian languages of aspiration and transcendence. As Chapter 4 illustrates, this dialectic is more than merely a characteristic of the poems' tone. It is an expression, within the structure of Larkin's vocabulary, of his divided response to the world: it mirrors and vitalizes a continual debate between hopeful romantic yearning and disillusioned pragmatism.

3

THE NOVELS

Larkin's period of delay and difficulty in finding his own voice as a poet was one of ease and confidence in prose. While still writing derivative and unformed poems, he published two original and self-possessed novels – and the first of them, *Jill*, appeared in 1946 when he was only 24. The second, *A Girl in Winter*, came out the following year.

Larkin has said that he was brought up on 'the kind of critical attitude you used to get in *Scrutiny*', which encouraged him to regard novels as 'rather poetic things',[61] and he has referred to his own as 'over-sized poems'.[62] But in fact the poeticisms of both novels are checked, in varying degrees, by other expectations he had of the form: 'A very crude difference between novels and poetry', he has argued, 'is that novels are about other people and poetry is about yourself.'[63] That is to say, by writing prose he escaped the romantic subjectivism he associated with poetry, and anticipated his later insistence that a writer's first obligations are to satisfy a 'pleasure-seeking audience'.[64] As he admitted himself: 'I think that when I began to write more characteristic poetry, I'd found how to make poems as readable as novels.'[65]

Jill and *A Girl in Winter* have received much less attention than Larkin's poetry and, for the last twenty-five years at least, have been placed in its shadow. But they are both novels that discuss Larkin's lasting preoccupations profoundly and at length, and they provide a graphic illustration of attitudes that determined his mature poetic language. There is, too, a revealing paradox in the sequence of their composition: *Jill*, which is predominantly realistic and naturalistic, was written when Larkin was under Yeats's sway but exhibits characteristics he came to admire in Hardy. *A Girl in Winter*, which is more Yeatsianly symbolic and more calculatingly vague, was written when Larkin was first discovering Hardy. To appreciate this is to challenge, again, the received notion of Larkin's development.

Larkin left Oxford in the summer of 1943, and when he began *Jill* shortly afterwards he immediately returned there in imagination. But, while the novel relies heavily on his memories of the university, it is careful to distinguish between its unillusioned author and its ignorant maladroit hero, John Kemp. Kemp is an 'undersized boy, eighteen years old' (*J*, p. 21), and undistinguished except that 'his silky hair, like pale thistle seed, was agreeable to look at' (*J*, p. 71). He is first introduced in a train travelling from Huddlesford to Oxford in the middle of the Second World War, about to begin his first term as an undergraduate reading English. He promptly reveals himself as painfully shy. Not daring to eat his sandwiches in front of strangers, he takes them to the lavatory. When someone tries the door, he crams them out through the window and returns to his seat – only to be embarrassed by offers of food from his fellow travellers. It is a set-piece of considerable importance, partly for the symbolic value discussed below (see pp. 45–7), and partly because it identifies insecurities that are to determine the course of Kemp's term at Oxford. It reveals him as frightened, inexperienced and – by reason of his coming from a northern industrial town – exiled from his environment, kind and class.

This isolation is intensified as soon as Kemp enters his college room, which he has been given to share with another undergraduate, Christopher Warner. Warner's minor-public-school swagger and social confidence first horrify Kemp and then impress him. They provide protection and, by appealing to a latent snobbishness, encourage him to assert himself. Another northern scholar, Whitbread, is the main cause of these brittle feelings of superiority, but by scorning him Kemp only deepens his own loneliness. He cannot belong to Warner's world – no matter how much he might want to – and deliberately cuts himself off from Whitbread's dour reminder of the past. From the evidence of a long flashback to Kemp's home and schooldays, it is easy to see why. His kindly but uncomprehending parents and his hardworking schoolmaster have made his life honest and worthy, but dull. By comparison, Warner's selfishnesses at least seem glamorous – even when Kemp has heard Warner insulting him, and knows that his isolation is absolute. 'After all', he realizes, 'he was on his own; he had failed, utterly and ignominiously failed to weave himself into the lives of these people. As he had feared, the door had swung open again and he was alone again, doubly alone' (J, p. 114).

In the absence of a real society, Kemp is driven to fabricate one. He invents an imaginary girl, Jill, referring to her first as a sister and then as a friend. Since Jill's creation occurs on the spur of the moment, as a proposed means of capturing Warner's attention, the formation of her identity and character begins uncertainly. But, once he has placed her at a school (Willow Gables), given her an age (15), a surname (Bradley) and friends, she is definite enough to admire. In fact Kemp falls in love with her – not that he admits it until later. He sends her letters, keeps what he pretends is her diary, and writes a short story in her name. But, for all its ingenuity, Jill's life is a vulnerable construction. Its most serious weakness is Kemp's wish to translate his illusions into actual conditions, and when he encounters a girl in a bookshop who seems to 'be' Jill he precipitates a disaster. The girl seems to embody the innocence he cherished in Jill, and, although he understands the perils of seeking to realize this quality in the tainted social world, he cannot resist the temptation. To start with, the girl's character appears flawless because it remains unknown. Kemp despairingly searches for her around Oxford but sees her only occasionally and fleetingly. Then after another sighting he follows her to the very place he least expects to find her, and would most like her to avoid: his own room, where Warner is

41

giving a party. The girl turns out to be a cousin of Warner's girlfriend Elizabeth, and her name is Gillian – though she refuses to be called Jill.

Having admitted the possibility that Jill could be found in life, Kemp is immediately obsessed by Gillian. Once he has crossed the boundary between a self-contained fantasy and the autonomous external world, he becomes the servant of an ideal he originally controlled. And, while the love he felt for Jill could afford to be as innocent as herself, his love for Gillian cannot help but be strongly sexual and deeply disturbing. Elizabeth, however, who is acting as Gillian's chaperon, is determined to protect her charge, and when Kemp invites Gillian to tea he is firmly disappointed. 'I think it would be better if she didn't come,' Elizabeth tells him. 'When she told me, I thought it was some kind of a joke you or someone were trying to play. . . . But even if it isn't, I'm afraid it's not possible for her to come. I should have thought you'd have guessed that' (J, p. 201).

Kemp is prevented from brooding for too long on the implications of this rebuff by another and more literally destructive intervention. Whitbread tells him that Huddlesford has been bombed, and Kemp hurries home to enquire after his parents' safety. They and their house have survived intact, but it is a dismal homecoming nevertheless. Huddlesford provokes a feeling of isolation which exactly and painfully parallels his situation at Oxford: although he feels 'dependent on [his parents] for ever' (J, p. 214), the raid has dramatized his distance from them and his past. His home town now looks 'like the ruins of an age over and done with' (J, p. 215), and in it, as at university, Kemp is marooned between two worlds, two classes, and two kinds of attitude to experience; but before leaving for Oxford again he at least allows himself the luxury of contemplating a fresh start:

> The town meant no more to him now, and so it was destroyed: it seemed symbolic, a kind of annulling of his childhood. The thought excited him. It was as if he had been told: all the past is cancelled: all the suffering connected with

42

that town, all your childhood, is wiped out: . . . you are no longer governed by what has gone before. (*J*, p. 219)

When Kemp reaches Oxford, he is spurred to resolve his relationship with Gillian by this new sense of freedom. His decision to act is strengthened, too, by another unlooked-for change in his relationship with his past. Crouch, his former schoolmaster, comes to visit him – and, instead of seeming the helpful mentor that Kemp had always imagined, he proves to be self-seeking and opportunistic. Kemp has nowhere left to turn for comfort except the future, but lacks the self-knowledge to govern it wisely. His dilemma is worsened by the fact that most of his hopes are invested in Gillian, who provokes him to extreme bouts of ignorant impetuosity. It is the final and most severe of these fits that ends the novel. After an evening of steadily deepening drunkenness, Kemp attempts to find his way to a party, and stumbles on Gillian, Elizabeth and Warner during his search. The result is a catastrophic attempt to realize his ideal: 'John stood back. In the weak light his face was quite expressionless. Everything seemed at that moment clear and restful. As Jill came level, he took her quietly in his arms and kissed her' (*J*, p. 239). Kemp's only rewards for this desperate boldness are to be assaulted by Warner, to be flung into a fountain, and to develop bronchial pneumonia (*J*, p. 240). As he lies in the college sickroom, the lessons he began to learn on his visit to Huddlesford return with renewed force. In his feverish dreams a series of incidents from his life with Jill and Gillian return and torment him – some accurate, some distorted. But in spite of their variety they all teach the same things: that, no matter how vigorously he might exercise his power to choose, he would be wrong to expect 'control over the maddened surface of things' (*J*, p. 243); and that 'love died, whether fulfilled or unfulfilled' (*J*, p. 242).

Even a rapid summary of *Jill*'s plot is enough to show that the novel explores an issue that dominates Larkin's three mature collections: the need to be less deceived. But, having established this, his commentators invariably pass on. David

Timms, for instance, who is better on Larkin's prose than most, is content to confine himself to investigating what he calls 'our tendency to make fantasies, and the dangers into which it leads us'.[66] But this theme depends for much of its force on two other aspects of the book, which complement it but which have gone unregarded. The first is that *Jill* is, in a sense, a kind of cryptic literary manifesto. It is a novel about writing, about discovering a literary personality, and about the sorts of consolation that art can provide. These things are interwoven in the creation of the heroine: as Kemp brings her to life in a short story, diary and letters, he adopts various literary personalities and tests the various kinds of protection they offer from the social world. Among others, he tries the aesthetic-dandyish, the touristic-appreciative and the boorish good-living:

> we came out of the Bull into the dark when Eddy had one of his boring fits of bravado, during which he keeps badgering one to dare him to do something. In the end I said: All right, Eddy, go into the Union there and smash the first glass door you see. All right, he said, and straightway disappeared into porch [*sic*]. None of us had the least idea he'd be crazy enough to do it, but just as we were assuring each other that he'd come out in the end with his tail between his legs, there came the most fearsome sound of breaking glass. (The Union, as I dare say you know, is a seedy Gothic place full of decayed clergymen.) (*J*, p. 134)

Kemp's styles are ways of disguising his failures and compensating for his disappointments. Without writing, he would be nothing – a terrified prey to Warner's whims, and overlooked by all his contemporaries. The point is made throughout the novel, implicitly by Kemp's energy as a fantasizer, and explicitly by his vacuity in the social world. When he first reaches Oxford he has virtually no character at all, and is able to make his presence felt only by imitating other people. Going into a pub on one occasion,

He imagined himself saying in the future: 'D'you remember

that time we went to the Bull, old boy. In our first term? D'you know, that was really and truly the first time I'd ever seen the inside of a bar. . . .' ('Oh, come off it, old boy!') 'S'fact: My dear fellow, it's absolutely bloody gospel! Here, after you with the – whoops! Don't drown it. . . .' His voice would be rich and husked with tobacco. (*J*, p. 62)

The model here is Warner, and a few pages later when he attends a lecture it is Crouch, 'nodding his head wisely at intervals and making a few microscopic jottings, to be copied and expanded later' (*J*, p. 96).

While Kemp's writings are shown both to reflect and to compensate for his juvenile lack of character, they also allow him to nurture a dangerous idealism. And when he meets Gillian his attempts to transfer an imaginary 'hallucination of innocence' (*J*, p. 135) into a specific context are violently disruptive. But what crushes the hero is a liberation for his creator: by collapsing Kemp's illusory world, Larkin completes his own fictional one, and contradicts Kemp's view of the ways in which art consoles. Although Kemp is a kind of budding novelist within the novel – a creator of characters and narratives – his procedures are the opposite of the novel's itself. Where Kemp's prose projects illusions to compensate for uncertainties, Larkin's strips them away. Writing, the novel argues, is not a refuge but an action – an attempt to understand and control. To clinch its point, it keeps its own style scrupulously plain, observant and realistic.

Jill's self-consciousness is restrained: its language, structure and time-scheme are strictly traditional. For all its reserve, however, the book's preoccupation with deception produces at least one ambitious pattern of images and symbols. These are all, in one way or another, to do with food, and begin to assert themselves as soon as the novel begins. Kemp's reluctance to eat in front of his fellow travellers, and his embarrassment at being offered food when he has thrown his own sandwiches away, initiates a series of scenes in which food plays an important part, and which leave him – at least to start with –

'utterly humiliated' (*J*, p. 23). As soon as he reaches his room he finds that Warner has broken open a case of his own (Kemp's) tea-things, and is holding a party. Once again he is ostracized at what should be – and traditionally is – a moment of social harmony. Subsequently he is lonely throughout his college life, a considerable part of which is seen at hall during meals. By the time he first meets Whitbread (the name might prepare us for this) he has already come to associate food with repulsion: 'Whitbread's eagerness was embarrassing: it was like watching a man scouring his plate with a piece of bread' (*J*, p. 53).

Similar scenes abound in the first half of the novel (see *J*, pp. 32, 39, 49) – until he meets Gillian – and shed a keen light on Kemp's insecurity. The references to food amount to an exposition of awkward shyness about more than simply eating. They reveal uncertainty and ignorance about his character in general and its bodily functions in particular: they are, in other words, a means of expressing what is predominantly a sexual anxiety. Kemp spends a great deal of his time acting and reflecting on sexual motives but seldom identifies them as such. Usually they occur simply as unfocused longings – as, for instance, when Elizabeth has flirtatiously tied his bow-tie for him. 'Elizabeth filled his thoughts. Not only Elizabeth, but all that stretched beyond her – iridescent, tingling feelings that had not any obvious cause, shadowy wishes, and more shadowy dreams of fulfilment' (*J*, p. 100).

Once Kemp has encountered Gillian, he is forced to clarify the nature of his wants, and the novel's images of food change radically. They show him becoming either forceful and peremptory, or sensuously lavish. As soon as Kemp has followed Gillian to his and Warner's room, he steals a cake from Whitbread for her to eat (following the sexually confident Warner's example: Warner had already wrecked another undergraduate's room while searching for food). Later, when Kemp invites Gillian to tea, he prepares a feast for her which is the wartime, rationed equivalent of the meal Porphyro offers Madeline in Keats's 'The Eve of Saint Agnes': 'a number of fruit tarts, a jam roll and a sponge cake filled with jam, and a fruit cake' (*J*, p. 196); and, after a second shopping expedition, radishes, lettuces, and bread and butter. It is, of course, this seductive and excitedly described meal that Elizabeth prevents, thereby provoking the final drama of the novel. In this, too, food plays a prominent part. At the height of his drunkenness, Kemp disrupts Whitbread's room. It is an Amisian moment, but entirely in keeping with Larkin's switch from using food as a symbol of sexually derived anxiety to one of sexually motivated action. At the tea party food was intended to seduce Gillian; here it is deployed as an expression of his angry disappointment:

> He opened the cupboard door, and, taking out the jam pot, put a large spoonful of jam on each of the open books lying on the desk. Then he snapped them shut. The rest of the jam he ladled on to the back of the fire, scraping out the pot thoroughly and licking the spoon. There was a nearly new pat of butter in the cupboard, too, and this he unwrapped from its paper and cut in half, putting each half into the toes of Whitbread's slippers. Then he filled the pockets of the jackets hanging in the bedroom with sugar and tea. In one of them there was a pound note with a slip of paper bearing its number pinned to it, and he put that in his own pocket book. As an afterthought, he poured Whitbread's milk into the coal scuttle and lit the fire. (*J*, p. 230)

There are two main causes for Kemp's sexual reticence – or, to put it another way, two reasons why the novel transforms sexual preoccupations into images of food, rather than discussing them openly. For one thing, Kemp is determined that Warner and his associates must know nothing about his fantasy life. If they discover it, it will immediately be destroyed by their mockery. For another, Kemp is tormented by the 'enormous disparity . . . between his imagination and what actually happened' in sexual relations (*J*, p. 170). When he has only the imaginary Jill to admire, he can persuade himself that it is innocence he cherishes; but when Gillian appears he is plunged into the world of actual desire. Whether he sleeps with her or not, she is still tyrannized by his attentions, and this makes Kemp realize that his emotions are, in essence, the same as those he finds confusing and often repugnant in other people. It is, again, when Elizabeth flirts with him that he appreciates this most clearly: 'A horrible embarrassment tingled and shuddered inside him, that what he had imagined to be his most secret feeling was almost cynically common' (*J*, p. 109). The same point is made with crude force in a passage Larkin cut from the novel when revising it for publication in 1964: Kemp 'was shocked to discover that, like Christopher [Warner], he was after a woman'.[67]

Later in this same excised passage Kemp reflects that 'he had none of Christopher's self-possession, confident knowledgeableness and amusement when faced with what he theatrically called "the last step". As he was not given to erotic fancyings he had almost deliberately left this part blank.'[68] The novel's complex use of food imagery demonstrates that 'erotic fancyings' are precisely what spur a good deal of Kemp's behaviour. In his fantasy life with Jill he is too quickly embarrassed and inexperienced to admit more than a longing for innocent company, but after Gillian's appearance his feelings are easily identified. Once this has occurred, it is only a matter of time before he precipitates the novel's physical crisis: kissing Gillian. In itself this is a relatively slight sin against modesty, but its significance for Kemp is immense. (Apart from being told it makes her cry, we are left to imagine the effect on Gillian.) In his sickroom, the kiss returns to haunt him:

As his temperature rose, untruths took their place quite naturally among these recollections. One of the earliest was that they were lying together on the floor of some room in each other's arms. He could feel her lips pressed against his, but he could not feel the rest of her. He could not feel her with his body at all. He hugged her harder, rolling desperately against her, but it was all nothing, he could not feel her at all. Everything was confined to the mouth and he would wake up with burning lips. (*J*, p. 24)

This is the novel's ironic climax – ironic because it is simply another kind of illusion, a nightmare, replacing Kemp's original fantasies. Its conclusions, however, are tried and proven, and part of their power derives from their connection with the book's earlier symbolic patterning. *Jill*'s preoccupation with food is here changed into a different kind of obsession, but one that is nevertheless also oral. It is an important point because it highlights and concludes Kemp's development throughout the novel from shy 'unfocused' feelings to explicit self-awareness. Although he is still in a dream, he has clarified the nature of his impulses, wishes and desires. He has acquired self-knowledge, and thereby achieved the condition to which all Larkin's speakers aspire. This represents a kind of consolation, but it does not release him from his predicament: while he has escaped the frustrations of fantasy, he has also confronted the certainty of exclusion, disappointment and loss.

*

Larkin's second novel, *A Girl in Winter* (1947), reaches precisely the same conclusion. After a long and painful process of self-discovery, the distresses of self-deception give way to unavoidable disillusionment. There are striking similarities, too, between the social isolation of its heroine, Katherine Lind, and Kemp's. But, where Kemp is shy and peripheral at Oxford, Katherine is lonely and isolated in England generally. The Second World War is, again, partly to blame: in *Jill* the bombing dramatized Kemp's separation from his past; in *A Girl in Winter* the war has forced Katherine – before the novel opens – to leave her unspecified European country of origin and seek safety in England. After a year, she has found work as an assistant in a provincial library; but the library staff as a whole, and its mean-minded head Mr Anstey in particular, repeatedly remind her that 'she was foreign and had no proper status there' (*GW*, p. 25). It is, in fact, her second visit to England; as a schoolgirl she spent a summer vacation with the family of her penfriend Robin Fennel. Now, after a long interval, they are in her mind again. She has happened to notice that a child of the daughter Jane has died, and she has written a letter of sympathy. When the narrative's first section begins, she is awaiting a reply.

At this early stage, information about Katherine's past is fragmentary, partly because most of her attention is commanded by the present. One of her fellow library assistants, Miss Green, has toothache, and Katherine is asked to take care of her. After visiting a dentist, the couple call at Katherine's flat, where a letter from Robin is waiting. It reveals that he is about to arrive:

> This she had not expected. Whatever else he had said, she would have had time to think, to make herself ready: but at this moment it was nearly twelve-fifteen, and Robin Fennel was coming towards this room and her like a bead sliding on a string. Why this alarmed her she had no idea. But she was nearly panic-stricken. (*GW*, p. 60)

No sooner has Katherine been recalled to her own affairs than she is forcibly withdrawn from them. When buying some aspirin from a chemist, she mistakes a stranger's handbag for Miss Green's and innocently brings it home. A letter in the bag, written in handwriting reminiscent of Mr Anstey's, indicates that its owner is called Miss Parbury. Miss Green querulously sends Katherine out, away from a possible rendezvous with Robin, to solve the muddle.

These oscillations between past and present, between reflection and action, cease in the second section of the narrative. As the adult, bewildered Katherine is travelling towards Miss Parbury, attention is concentrated exclusively on the young Katherine during her first visit to England. (The novel's elliptical title suppresses the fact that it refers to a woman in winter remembering being a girl in summer.) Time, which in the first and last sections is always hurrying events out of the characters' control, now passes languorously. When staying with the Fennels, Katherine can 'almost feel [the days] passing slowly, luxuriously, like thick cream pouring from a silver jug' (*GW*, p. 101). This is partly the result of her physical circumstances – a spell of hot weather and rural seclusion – but it is also a revelation of her state of mind. Because her English is uncertain and the country is strange to her, she finds herself in a state of prolonged disorientation. England, and what happens to her there, is a dream – palpable and new, but always impregnated with a sense of unreality. And because it seems illusory it encourages her to develop illusions of her own. Robin is their obvious focus. Even before coming to England she has lazily speculated on his suitability as an ideal friend, but her interest has always been overcome by his remoteness. When she is actually with him, she begins to idolize him – although his sister Jane is invariably in attendance as a chaperon. Katherine 'felt, as she felt ever since she had first seen his photograph, that he could, if he wished, say something that would be more important to her than anything she had ever heard' (GW, pp. 101–2). But Robin says nothing of the sort; he is merely well mannered and considerate, to the point at which Katherine suspects he is deliberately misrepresenting himself. She is left 'with the absurd feeling that the most important person, her real friend, had not yet appeared' (GW, p. 90). This puzzles Katherine but also entices her. The more rigorously Robin maintains his reserve, the more she wants to break it down – and when he takes her out punting, and saves her from lurching into the water, she realizes that she is in love with him:

> Katherine sank down on the cushions, trembling from rage, fright, and embarrassment. The bright, almost metallic contact when he had gripped her sharply wiped away all traces of self-deception. She knew she wanted to lie with her head in his lap, to have him comfort her: she knew equally that this was not going to happen partly because he had no interest in her, and partly because Jane was specifically there to prevent it. She sat blushing. (GW, pp. 125–6)

This unfulfilled awkwardness – an embarrassed version of Stephen and Maggie's river journey in *The Mill on the Floss* – forces Katherine into self-awareness. Jane has already bluntly told her that Robin is 'ordinary, down to the last button' (GW,

p. 107), but she has always resisted this possibility. Even when she cannot help noticing his dullness, she enshrines it as a 'barren perfection' (*GW*, p. 109). In the punt, however, at the very moment that her feelings for him are most conscious and definite, Robin is unmistakably disappointing. She cannot overlook the gulf between her ideal vision of him and his indifference to her. Shortly afterwards, when Katherine discovers that it was in fact Jane and not Robin who suggested that she should stay with the family, her self-deception is destroyed altogether: 'she saw how fatally obvious it all was. For two weeks she had exercised her imagination in building up theories based on the fact that Robin had invited her, and trying to hide from herself the dissatisfaction she felt with them' (*GW*, p. 147). When Katherine's ill-founded infatuation collapses, it brings down the romance of her surroundings with it. Robin and Jane are no more than 'two unremarkable young English people ... in their well-appointed house' (*GW*, p. 155), the weather begins to break, and the indolent, slow, uneventful pace of her time is quickened into a rush of incidents. Jack Stormalong, a young fast-talking friend of the Fennels, comes to stay and deposes Katherine from her position of exclusively cherished guest. His visit crashingly recalls her to the familiar world of boredom and ordinariness, and also precipitates two events on her last night in England which confirm the end of her illusions. Driven out of the house by Jack's interminable talk, Katherine goes to the punt, intending to take it out for a final elegiac trip. Unexpectedly she is joined by Robin, who takes the opportunity to give her the first sign of his affection. But, rather than confirming Katherine's original wish, his performance is ridiculous, inept and humiliating:

> He ducked his head and kissed her inexpertly with tight lips, as if dodging something that swept above their heads. It was not a bit like lovemaking, and she never thought of it as such till afterwards. He kept his face hidden against her hair. At the end of this unfathomable interval, he shivered, and the shiver changed to a short scrambling shudder, almost an

abortive attempt to climb on her; then he slowly relaxed. Still he would not look her in the face. In the end he released her, carelessly. (*GW*, p. 173)

Robin's kiss confirms the disparity between romantic aspirations and actual circumstances. It represents exactly the same lesson that Kemp learns after kissing Gillian – and, like that encounter, it is mercilessly corroborated by subsequent events. In the closing lines of the second section, Jane informs Katherine that she has agreed to marry Jack. Jane, having no romantic illusions, is at least spared the pain of losing them, but what she settles for instead has its own miseries: a marriage to escape boredom at home, and an admittedly deficient love for her husband.

The bleak conclusion implied by this second section is confirmed by the third, in which Katherine resumes her wintry journey to Miss Parbury. The visit is unexpectedly traumatic, largely because Katherine discovers (from the letter in the handbag) that Mr Anstey is courting Miss Parbury. It is a drastic coincidence, and suggests a good deal of desperation on Larkin's part to convey his moral point. The letter not only means that Mr Anstey is 'no longer a sharply-cut target for loathing' (*GW*, p. 189) but also reminds Katherine of the dingy, anxious uncertainties of affection. In a long, speculative passage about the value and purpose of human relationships, Katherine resolves to live without them, since they bring only pain and disappointment:

> She no longer felt that she was exalted or made more worthy if she could spin her friendships to incredible subtlety and fineness. It was something she had tired of doing. And what had replaced it? Here she was at a loss. She was not sure if anything had replaced it.
>
> She was not sure if anything would replace it. (*GW*, pp. 183–4)

To deny love means opting for dissatisfaction and obscurity. But, while this involves a cruel suppression of hope, it also offers (admittedly reductive) opportunities for self-preservation. In the third section of *A Girl in Winter* this ambivalence is carefully explored. By the time Robin appears, Katherine has returned from Miss Parbury to the library, and has been further convinced of the value of keeping herself to herself. The demands of Miss Parbury's invalid mother, Miss Green's gossip and Mr Anstey's offensive anger have all thwarted her recent attempts to put even a little faith in other people. Robin's behaviour is a rebuttal of a different kind. He has slipped away from training camp with the intention of sleeping with Katherine, and his tipsy, badgering kisses threaten to damage the memory of her childhood stay with the Fennels. Until Robin's arrival, she had managed to retain a belief that the holiday, for all its disappointments and short-comings, was nevertheless the 'only period of her life that had not been spoiled by later events, and she found she could draw upon it hearteningly' (*GW*, p. 185). Now she is forced to realize that he is as he always was – 'still nearly a chance acquaintance to her' (*GW*, p. 232). The more he pesters her, the more completely he destroys her version of the past, and the less chance of happiness he allows.

Her final indifference is simply a hopeless kind of charity, and she can afford to give it only because she knows her isolation is complete: 'He could not touch her. It would be no more than doing him an unimportant kindness, that would be overtaken by oblivion in a few days' (*GW*, p. 243). This is exactly the same conclusion that *Jill* describes in Kemp's realization that 'love died, whether fulfilled or unfulfilled', and, like the earlier novel, it insists that the benefits of unillusioned independence are limited. To be less deceived often has to be its own reward; self-knowledge allows fulfilment of a kind, but it is invariably accompanied by a bitter memory of pleasures and opportunities that have been irretrievably and unforgettably lost.

Although *A Girl in Winter* and *Jill* have almost identical themes, they arrive at their conclusions by radically different means. Where *Jill* is precise in its placing of characters and background, *A Girl in Winter* is deliberately vague; where *Jill* is unwaveringly – sometimes excessively – naturalistic and realistic, *A Girl in Winter* is 'a Virginia Woolf–Henry Green kind of novel';[69] and, where *Jill* incorporates its symbolical structures into an empirical framework, *A Girl in Winter* matches its actual observations with well-advertised symbolic intentions. It is these qualities that John Bayley summarized when he called *A Girl in Winter* 'one of the finest and most sustained prose poems in the language',[70] and they are immediately apparent in the opening pages. The first section, like the second and third, is prefaced by a brooding meditation on the weather which is to dominate it. Life and scenery are cast into distinct but nevertheless archetypal symbolic forms. 'People' rather than individuals are described: 'There had been no more snow during the night, but because the frost continued so that the drifts lay where they had fallen, people told each other there was more to come' (*GW*, p. 11). Elsewhere on the first page Larkin refers to 'People who lay ill in bed' (*GW*, p. 11) and 'People [who] were unwilling to get up' (*GW*, p. 11). The blanketing snow deprives places of particular features as well: landscape is simply a matter of representative fields, villages, railway lines, factories and cities – everywhere 'so white and still it might have been a formal painting' (*GW*, p. 11). This generalizing technique is interrupted, once the action proper begins, by a particular, banal conversation between library assistants, and the contrast is one that occurs in different forms elsewhere in the novel. The interweaving of Katherine's childhood memories of the Fennels, and her grim progress with Miss Green to the dentist, is another obvious example. Clearly, it is a device that anticipates Larkin's alternations between two kinds of language in much later poems like 'Vers de Société' – and its purpose is very much the same. The switches between 'poetic' prose and realistic documentation, like those between Yeatsian and Hardyesque dictions, continually alert the reader to differences between vague idealistic wishes and pragmatic considerations.

But the 'poetic' moments in *A Girl in Winter* do more than

simply encapsulate a spirit of romantic hopefulness; they also imply that it can never be fulfilled. All the novel's incidents of aspiration and contentment are either unreliably indistinct or unbelievably hyperbolic, and whatever human actions they describe are therefore also beautified but not to be trusted. Larkin's evocation of the weather is a case in point – the summer has 'every romantic backdrop ready to hand' (*GW*, p. 127). The Fennels' house has the same function. It is set in a village which is never named, and is persistently described in exaggeratedly pastoral terms:

> 'This is a wonderful place for growing things,' said Robin. 'See how sheltered it is, with the high wall on one side and these fruit trees on the other. And there you see it slopes pretty well due south down to the river, and catches all the sun.' (*GW*, p. 86)

Its qualities as a home are everywhere subordinate to its role as an emblem of potentially ideal but always elusive happiness. The river that flows along the foot of the garden is realized to the same effect. Only in the final pages is Katherine told it is the Thames, and – as with the village itself – its lack of particular detail ensures that symbolic values take precedence over naturalistic purposes. It is less a specific river than a means of escape from the confines of home, and a catalyst for dangerous emotions. A succession of unsettling scenes occurs on its unstable element: Jane and Robin have an argument, Katherine wakes up to the real nature of her feelings for Robin, and Robin and Katherine have their unsatisfactory kiss. The river provides a metaphor for the unstoppable passage of Katherine's time in England, a symbol of its mixed indolence and potency, and a medium for the whole quickly traversed range of her sexual experience – from incipient excitement to disappointment.

This emphasis on the general rather than the particular is also evident in the novel's treatment of character. Although Larkin carefully and clearly differentiates people and temperaments, he is also at pains to suggest that they are representative.

This applies to a number of minor characters, as well as to Robin and Katherine themselves. Mr Anstey, for instance, is stigmatized as a type: his fussy irritability and 'unbreakable belief that all things depended on him' (*GW*, p. 21) are escalated to make his menace seem larger than life, and yet also unreal; he is 'theatrical' (*GW*, p. 16), his outbursts are 'performances' (*GW*, p. 16), and his voice is one 'that might be used on the stage as typically insulting' (*GW*, p. 18). Katherine, on the other hand, is threatened and isolated by a lack of particularizing detail. Little is known about her background – her father is a silversmith, in what country is never revealed. Her name is apparently Scandinavian,[71] but her home is near the Rhine and has been invaded by the British. This lack of specific detail makes her unapproachable and means that she is condemned always to be an onlooker. In England everything she sees is affected with the same imprecision – the customs, the countryside and, in particular, Robin. Although she hankers to know his 'real personality', it is continually withheld. 'His actions rarely had anything stronger than the flavour of a motive around them' (*GW*, p. 87), she realizes early in their relationship; and later: 'There was something formal about him, as if he were a figure in an allegory' (*GW*, p. 172). The same might also be said of Katherine herself. Larkin continually confuses her immediate circumstances, with the result that her search for identity and workable absolute values are moved to a general plane and made to seem unreal. At the end of the novel, when Robin re-enters her life, he arouses the same uncertainties that dominated her childhood holiday:

> The day was already so unlike other days that it was beginning to resemble an odyssey in a dream: to find herself in strange places, looking for strange people, following out thin threads of coincidence – it was almost as if an enchantment had been put on her to keep her away from the only two places where Robin knew she might be. (*GW*, pp. 179–80)

A Girl in Winter is, as this passage says, 'an odyssey', a quest, beset by various kinds of deception. As in *Jill*, the only reliable

57

truths are certainties of disappointment, and the only way of coming to terms with them is not to expect anything else. Living, the novels suggest, necessarily involves cultivating a self-protective pessimism. *A Girl in Winter* approaches this conclusion much more knowingly than *Jill* and – via its symbolic enlargements – with much greater determination to demonstrate it as a universal rather than a merely personal truth. But it is this which makes the novel, for all its immaculate care of writing, less compelling and forceful than *Jill*. *Jill* has all the faults of overwriting likely to exist in a novel written by a 21-year-old, but it is less self-conscious in its symbolic strategies, and more easily capable of being surprised by the world. Its language is less scrupulous but more energetic, and its theme less fully developed but more shockingly discovered. *A Girl in Winter* is a beautifully constructed, funny and profoundly sad book, but its development of 'Virginia Woolf–Henry Green's strategies has an unignorably reductive effect. Although it juxtaposes passages of rarefied writing with close attention to the familiar, the two styles convey a uniformly bleak attitude to experience. In his three mature collections the realism exemplified by *Jill* and the symbolism that dominates *A Girl in Winter* are brought into a more intimate and fruitful connection. They create a dialectic between Larkin's recurrently pessimistic impulse and his irrepressible longing for fulfilment.

4

THE POEMS

Larkin has often been regarded as a hopeless and inflexible pessimist. Eric Homberger has called him 'the saddest heart in the post-war supermarket',[72] Geoffrey Thurley has stressed his 'central dread of satisfaction',[73] and Charles Tomlinson has criticized his 'tenderly nursed sense of defeat'.[74] But these are all views that need to be re-examined if the range and resourcefulness of Larkin's poems are to be appreciated. Although he has done a good deal to project the image of himself as 'a Parnassian Ron Glum', he has always denied its complete accuracy. 'The impulse for producing a poem', he has said, 'is never negative; the most negative poem in the world is a very positive thing to have done.'[75] This is particularly evident in bitterly angry or satirical poems like 'Naturally the Foundation will Bear Your Expenses', 'Send No Money', 'Homage to a Government', 'The Card-Players' or 'This Be The Verse': their rage or contempt is always checked by the assuaging energy of their language and the satisfactions of their articulate formal control. But, even when the mitigating function of language is less obvious, Larkin's poems are not as narrowly circumscribed as has often been claimed. By looking at a few of his recurrent themes, it is possible to see that his pessimism is not axiomatic, his attitude to death is in marked contrast to Hardy's, and his hope of deriving comfort from social and natural rituals is resilient. And, by examining his use of symbolist devices, it is clear that his poems describe a number of moments which – qualifiedly but indubitably – manage to transcend the flow of contingent time altogether.

What seems to have misled Larkin's critics into regarding him as uniformly depressed is the fact that he clearly has no faith in inherited and reliable absolutes. But, in so far as this means that individuals must discover and develop their own internal resources, his poems have an unmistakably affirmative aspect. It is one that Larkin has pointed out in Hardy's work too, where 'sensitivity to suffering and awareness of the causes of pain' are associated with 'superior spiritual character'.[76] The most obvious cause of this necessary self-reliance is the lack of the most time-honoured absolute of all: religion. As 'Church Going' indicates, Larkin's dilemma is not whether to believe in God but what to put in God's place; he is concerned in the poem, he has said, with 'going to church, not religion. I tried to suggest this by the title – and the union of the important stages of human life – birth, marriage and death – that going to church represents.'[77] It describes, in other words, a strictly secular faith; his speculations about what churches will become when they fall 'completely' rather than partially 'out of use' lead him to a conclusion in which the fear of death and the loss of religious belief are counteracted by an ineradicable faith in human and individual potential:

> A serious house on serious earth it is,
> In whose blent air all our compulsions meet,
> Are recognized, and robed as destinies.
> And that much never can be obsolete,
> Since someone will forever be surprising
> A hunger in himself to be more serious,
> And gravitating with it to this ground,
> Which, he once heard, was proper to grow wise in,
> If only that so many dead lie around. (*LD*, p. 29)

Much the same point is made in a more recent, and apparently more desolate poem, 'The Building' (*HW*, pp. 24–6). Like 'Church Going', it is set in a post-Christian era, at least from the speaker's point of view. When he looks down from the hospital, he sees a stubbornly 'locked church'. Religion is closed to him – it can do nothing to bring the world's 'loves' and 'chances' within reach, and cannot provide comfort, as it once did, in the face of death. But, in place of what he has called, in 'Aubade', Christianity's 'vast moth-eaten musical brocade',[78] Larkin hesitantly supplies two consolations. The first is the hospital itself. By admitting that 'its powers' at least have the potential to 'Outbuild cathedrals' and contravene 'The coming dark', he registers the legitimacy of hope at the same time as he rejects the support of the church. The hope, of course, is not that death will be everlastingly withheld from the 'unseen congregations' of patients, but that it will be kept temporarily at bay and that they will have time and suitable circumstances in which to prepare themselves to meet it. The second and similarly qualified consolation is represented by the visitors who come each evening 'With wasteful, weak, prop- itiatory flowers.' These offerings are as ambiguous as the building itself. On the one hand they are pathetically in- adequate props in the 'struggle to transcend / The thought of dying', on the other they are manifestations of a perennial and courageous attempt to do so. Their weakness cannot altogether obliterate the value of the spirit in which they are brought.

In 'Church Going' and 'The Building', as in 'The Explosion', Larkin looks to familiar social and natural rituals for the inspiration that might formerly have come from the church. In other poems he concentrates on the rewards of the natural world more exclusively – but, as 'Cut Grass' or 'Forget What Did' illustrate, they provide an equivalently ambiguous com- fort. 'The Trees' is another example:

> The trees are coming into leaf
> Like something almost being said;
> The recent buds relax and spread,
> Their greenness is a kind of grief.
>
> Is it that they are born again
> And we grow old? No, they die too.
> Their yearly trick of looking new
> Is written down in rings of grain.

> Yet still the unresting castles thresh
> In fullgrown thickness every May.
> Last year is dead, they seem to say,
> Begin afresh, afresh, afresh. (*HW*, p. 12)

'The Trees' denies that nature allows people to believe in their immortality. But, while this denial provokes the same vulnerability as that produced by lack of faith in orthodox religion, there are positive aspects as well. In spite of their steadily increasing age, the trees do at least 'seem' to return unchanged each year, and invite the speaker to follow their example and begin his life 'afresh'. Their towering solidity (they are like 'castles') dwarfs his knowledge of mortality. And this is their consolation: their rejuvenation confirms his human potential, without deceiving him into thinking that it can last for ever. Larkin, here as elsewhere, sees through appearances at the same time as he seizes on them.

That said, he is much less interested in nature for its own sake than for the opportunities it offers to moralize about the human condition. It is this which accounts for what Donald Davie has uncharitably called his 'imperiousness towards the non-human';[79] it is in fact not imperiousness but an admission that the natural world is beautiful, restorative and necessary, yet also vulnerable and transient. 'Going, Going' makes the point forcefully:

> It seems, just now,
> To be happening so very fast;
> Despite all the land left free
> For the first time I feel somehow
> That it isn't going to last,
>
> That before I snuff it, the whole
> Boiling will be bricked in
> Except for the tourist parts –
> First slum of Europe: a role
> It won't be so hard to win,
> With a cast of crooks and tarts. (*HW*, p. 22)

As poems like 'MCMXIV' and 'Sad Steps' show, the 'celestial recurrences' of the natural cycle are subject to social disruption and personal disaffection, as well as industrial vandalism. But this only confirms their importance as symbols of constancy and hope. Usually their delicacy is emphasized by Larkin's choosing to write about them in fragile lyric forms. In 'Show Saturday', though, their implicit human lessons are treated more expansively. The poem moves towards its climax with an intensely affectionate deliberation, cataloguing the events of the show, transforming precise observation into a long, rapt epiphany: bales 'Like great straw dice', 'blanch leeks like church candles' and 'pure excellences' of scones and eggs and vegetables. They represent an ideal – in themselves and in the style used to describe them – of familiar Englishness:

Let it stay hidden there like strength, below
Sale-bills and swindling; something people do,
Not noticing how time's rolling smithy-smoke
Shadows much greater gestures; something they share
That breaks ancestrally each year into
Regenerate union. Let it always be there. (HW, p. 39)

There are, of course, regenerate unions more particularly concerned with people themselves, rather than with things, or the things 'people do'. On the face of it, social relations are given short shrift by Larkin – largely because of his view that circumstances continually drive people back into isolation. While this has the advantage of encouraging personal autonomy, it also has an unavoidable danger: that the stronghold of the self will become walled with egoism as it battles to survive. Any commitment to the social world will be extremely wary, and made less for prospective pleasure than from a fear that staying at home will be unbearable. 'Vers de Société' is a striking example. The speaker realizes that the people he will meet at the Warlock-Williamses' party are likely to be '*a crowd of craps*', but eventually decides to go as a way of escaping himself:

> The time is shorter now for company,
> And sitting by a lamp more often brings
> Not peace, but other things.
> Beyond the light stand failure and remorse
> Whispering *Dear Warlock-Williams: Why, of course –*
>
> (*HW*, p. 36)

This conflict between the demands of society and its probable disappointments acquires a special poignancy in the more intimate context of his love poems. 'Faith Healing' movingly summarizes their common preoccupation:

> In everyone there sleeps
> A sense of life lived according to love.
> To some it means the difference they could make
> By loving others, but across most it sweeps
> As all they might have done had they been loved.
>
> (*WW*, p. 15)

Apparently Larkin's 'everyone' is bound to be disappointed: all people are either unloving or unloved. And their distress is intensified by the clarity with which they envisage how love 'ought to be'. In 'Love Songs in Age', typically, it is the 'bright incipience' which promises 'to solve, and satisfy, / And set unchangeably in order' (*WW*, p. 12). It is the triumphant justification for existence, and its most potent reward. But, precisely because its possible benefits are so great, the opportunities for realizing them are small. Sex is often disruptive and miserably disillusioning ('Deceptions', 'Dry Point'); the fascination of individuals wears thin ('Places, Loved Ones'); and the self is either sickeningly unworthy ('If, My Darling') or unluckily inept ('Wild Oats', 'Annus Mirabilis').

None of Larkin's poems registers the achievement of complete calm success in love, and even those that come closest are heavily qualified. 'Broadcast', for instance, for all its loving attentiveness, leaves its speaker in the dark, 'desperate', and unable to discover the addressee's distinct individuality. 'Wedding Wind', too, in spite of its excitement and fulfilment, offsets its 'happiness' with a barrage of incredulous questions and an admission that the speaker is 'sad' because other people and animals cannot share her contentment. The same kind of ambivalence exists in another of Larkin's poems which seems to break his general rule of disappointment, 'An Arundel Tomb'. Throughout, Larkin carefully weighs losses against profits, without denying the power and fact of affection. On one hand love is merely a theoretical possibility; on the other it does, literally, have the last word. More important, because neither half of the balance is allowed to dominate, he is able to create an effect of still – but not stony – composure. It is an equipoise that suggests the only love acceptable to him is one that knows how much threatens its existence. He realizes that the effigies 'lie in stone' – that their faithfulness is a deception – and also admits that for them to be shown holding hands at all is nothing more than 'A sculptor's sweet commissioned grace'.[80] But while the tomb may represent an 'attitude', a 'lie', it has become a kind of truth by virtue of having survived. Larkin contemplates its durable witness of faith and love, 'hoping it might be so' in his own and all lives:

> The stone fidelity
> They hardly meant has come to be
> Their final blazon, and to prove
> Our almost-instinct almost true:
> What will survive of us is love. (*WW*, p. 46)

Love, in theory at least, offers the ideal solution to Larkin's isolation in a world without reliably comforting absolutes. In the place of religion and romantic theories of childhood's or nature's beneficence, he cherishes the sanctity of personal relationships. But, far from being the trusted salvation that earlier twentieth-century writers – particularly the Bloomsbury Group – sometimes imagined, Larkin persistently explores the gap between what he expects of love and what it provides.

Comforts that are not readily given by love can sometimes be discovered in a less glamorous form of social commitment:

work. Occasionally Larkin's critics have identified the daily grind as a major cause of his discontent – largely because of 'Toads':

> Why should I let the toad *work*
>   Squat on my life?
> Can't I use my wit as a pitchfork
>   And drive the brute off? (*LD*, p. 32)

Characteristically, though, the poem takes the form of a debate between two sides of his personality – with the rebellious, freebooting, anti-authoritarian aspect having the first say. By the end of the poem his more orthodox and self-critical instincts have asserted themselves:

> For something sufficiently toad-like
>   Squats in me too;
> Its hunkers are heavy as hard luck
>   And cold as snow
>
> And will never allow me to blarney
>   My way to getting
> The fame and the girl and the money
>   All at one sitting.
>
> I don't say, one bodies the other
>   One's spiritual truth;
> But I do say it's hard to lose either
>   When you have both. (*LD*, pp. 32–3)

After the first eight lucid stanzas, the last one seems disarmingly compacted. In fact it is a statement of what should by now be obvious: that working and not working complement one another. The compression itself forms a crucial part of the poem's meaning. It conveys a sense of being trapped in an argument, and of a deliberate, difficult effort at self-persuasion. At this relatively early stage in Larkin's career ('Toads' was first published in 1955), his internal debate is intensely active, with each point fiercely contested.

Much more recently, in 'Posterity' (*HW*, p. 27), Larkin has reintroduced these terms of argument. Although he is primarily concerned with the psychological and poetic results of disappointment in the poem, he investigates them in the context of work – and to appreciate this is to rescue 'Posterity' from the misunderstanding it has suffered. At first glance, it seems entirely scornful of academic life and methods as they are represented by its anti-hero Jake Balokowsky. Bruce Martin has said that it attacks 'the shallowness and intellectual hypocrisy of literary criticism',[81] David Timms has called it a 'slashingly satirical portrait',[82] and Clive James, in his discussion of 'Livings', has sneeringly said it is 'full of stuff that Balokowsky is bound to get wrong'.[83] But for all Balokowsky's caricatured absurdities – his jeans and sneakers, his abusive hip diction and his interest in Protest Theatre – it is the poem's point to draw certain parallels between his predicament and Larkin's own. They are both, in Balokowsky's reductively crude phrase, 'old-type *natural* fouled-up guys' – Larkin by his own admission in a large number of other poems, and Balokowsky as a result of 'Some slight impatience with his destiny'. Their disappointments, fears and sadnesses are not caused by 'kicks or something happening', but by leading a familiar and ordinary existence. Moreover, they both experience a similar tension between romantic longings and pragmatic needs. Where Larkin is habitually torn between revolt and orthodoxy, Balokowsky once entertained the thought of teaching 'school in Tel Aviv', before 'Myra' and the need for money drew him to his safe, tenured job and 'an air-conditioned cell at Kennedy'.

The more obvious sequel to 'Toads', 'Toads Revisited', resolves its arguments by playing down these tensions. The poem is convinced that freedom from work would bring – as isolation did in 'Vers de Société' – 'Not peace, but other things':

> give me my in-tray,
> My loaf-haired secretary,
> My shall-I-keep-the-call-in-Sir:
> What else can I answer,

When the lights come on at four
At the end of another year?
Give me your arm, old toad;
Help me down Cemetery Road. (*WW*, p. 19)

For all its unavoidable tedium, work helps to combat the thought of impending death, and the main reason for this is its very dailiness – the fact that its repetitive structures allow Larkin to feel palpably involved with life. It is not so much a routine as a ritual and, like all rituals, supportive. Work may be less glamorous than the ceremonies surrounding birth in 'Born Yesterday', or marriage in 'The Whitsun Weddings', or even social communion in 'Show Saturday', but it shares their essential qualities. Hence Larkin's irritation with 'romantic reviewers' who accuse his poems of depicting a 'uniquely dreary life': 'I'd like to know how . . . [they] spend their time. Do they kill a lot of dragons for instance?'[84]

But, while rituals offer some comfort in the face of death, they cannot – obviously – prevent its approach. 'Realisation of it rages out / In furnace-fear', Larkin says in 'Aubade', 'when we are caught without / People or drink' – or work, he might have added. From an unusually early age, death has been the rivetingly imagined fact that has forced him to limit his expectations of life. The note struck by the pretentious quatrain in *The North Ship* – 'This is the first thing / I have understood: / Time is the echo of an axe / Within a wood' (*NS*, p. 39) – has been repeated throughout his mature work, insistently and with gradually increasing clarity. In 'Aubade' itself – one of his most recently published poems – he is unprecedentedly straightforward:

I work all day, and get half drunk at night.
Waking at four to soundless dark, I stare.
In time the curtain-edges will grow light.
Till then I see what's really always there:
Unresting death, a whole day nearer now,
Making all thought impossible but how
And where and when I shall myself die.[85]

This kind of plainness testifies to a remarkable lack of self-deception. In other contexts, being less deceived has its own rewards – but death, in Larkin's view, is an utterly comfortless blank. The frequency and forcefulness with which he envisages its approach go a long way towards explaining why he is so often regarded as an unrelievedly pessimistic poet. The evidence of 'Going', 'Nothing To Be Said', 'The Building' and 'The Old Fools' makes it hard to think otherwise. They all confirm the categoric statement at the close of 'Dockery and Son':

> Life is first boredom, then fear.
> Whether or not we use it, it goes,
> And leaves what something hidden from us chose,
> And age, and then the only end of age. (WW, p. 38)

There is an obvious affinity between this attitude and one commonly adopted by Hardy. Both poets – not to mention other kindred spirits like Edward Thomas and A. E. Housman – are obsessed with the destructive passage of time, and similarly tend to divide past, present and future into distinct and discrete units. But, while Larkin sees them as being mutually exclusive, they are not mutually oblivious. The present in which his personae live and speak is continually embarrassed or thwarted by the past – which is brimming with missed opportunities – and is also mocked or intimidated by the future – which for all its promise is overshadowed by the memory of past disappointments. Their here-and-now is somewhere they long dreamed of, and will look back on with mingled sadness and nostalgia. Or, as 'Triple Time' puts it: the 'traditionally soured' present was once 'the future furthest childhood saw', and will be the past – 'a valley cropped by fat neglected chances / That we insensately forbore to fleece'. It is a theme he handles most grandly and philosophically at the end of 'Reference Back':

> Truly, though our element is time,
> We are not suited to the long perspectives

Open at each instant of our lives.
They link us to our losses: worse,
They show us what we have as it once was,
Blindingly undiminished, just as though
By acting differently we could have kept it so.

(*WW*, p. 40)

Although Larkin admits he cannot alter time's intransigence, let alone escape the fact of mortality, his poems are very far from being records of passive suffering. His response is certainly not Yeats's heroic struggle to rise above time, but neither is it Hardy's shoulder-shrugging acceptance of fate. And only in 'Wants' ('Beneath it all, desire of oblivion runs'; *LD*, p. 22) does he express anything like a romantic death wish. Normally, as in 'Aubade', he recoils in horror from the prospect of dying. His poems, in other words, have a profoundly moral character, which expresses itself in a need to control and manipulate life, rather than submit to a predetermined pattern of unsuccess – hence his emphasis on the necessity of choice. The power to choose is repeatedly highlighted as the most fulfilling of all human capabilities. As his poems explore the gulf between deception and clearsightedness, illusion and reality, solitude and sociability, they constantly discuss the need to decide on one or other of them: that is, not simply to notice the difference, but to make an active choice about which to adopt. The two parts of his poetic personality are constantly in negotiation with one another, animated by his conviction that – to borrow a phrase from 'Mr Bleaney' – 'how we live measures our own nature' (*WW*, p. 10). In 'The Old Fools', for instance (*HW*, pp. 19–20), one of the first and most appalling signs of death's advance is 'the power / Of choosing gone', and in 'The Building' (*HW*, pp. 24–6) the patients are pitied for – among other things – being 'at that vague age that claims / The end of choice'. Choosing, like everything else, is vulnerable to death, but Larkin's preoccupation with the thought of its loss is a measure of his commitment to life. He is much too conscious of possible deception to believe in the unshakeable rightness of any decision he might make, but he is similarly convinced that courting this danger is preferable to living a life determined by 'something hidden from us'. At worst the power of choosing is responsible for a life of compromise which, for all its frustrations, is still life. At best, it permits self-knowledge and fulfilment – as the young men of 'How Distant' discover. Larkin's celebration of their ability to enjoy the present, and start a new life, is one in which the word 'decisions' plays an important part:

> This is being young,
> Assumption of the startled century
>
> Like new store clothes,
> The huge decisions printed out by feet
> Inventing where they tread,
> The random windows conjuring a street. (*HW*, p. 31)

In 'How Distant' Larkin gives a rare glimpse of uncompromised achievement – though here as elsewhere it exists for people other than himself. This is both a source of irritation and a spur to imaginative release: the knowledge that life-enhancing opportunities are 'for others undiminished somewhere' prevents his poems from lapsing into the security of settled melancholy. And, even when fulfilment is less evident than in 'How Distant', he persistently offsets his knowledge of human limitations with his appreciation of human potential. It is a frail consolation, and yet by remorselessly delineating threats to faith, love and happiness he discovers these things in their most resilient form. But to deduce from this that he merely reckons it is better to live suffering losses than not to live at all is to draw too simple a conclusion. While it is true to say that he clings to life, no matter how unsatisfactory it might be, there is also a sense in which he views trials and tribulations as rewarding in themselves. This is not because he thinks – in the spirit of self-mortification – that suffering is intrinsically beneficial, but because like Hardy he believes that only by fully comprehending the fact and extent of suffering does any 'Catching of happiness' become possible. Appropriately, it is a point most clearly made in his own words on Hardy. He admits that Hardy's poetry shares his concern with 'time and the passing of time, love and the fading of love', but also affirms that it is 'a continual imaginative celebration of what is both the truest and the most important element in life, most important in the sense of most necessary to spiritual development.'[86]

*

It would be wrong to say that Larkin's emphasis on the potential and resilience of the human spirit cancelled out his pessimism. The point and value of rescuing the affirmative aspects of his work from neglect is not to make him seem a covertly optimistic poet but to expose the typical structure of his poems as a debate between hope and hopelessness, between fulfilment and disappointment. It is this argument that Larkin's use of symbolist techniques helps to dramatize; for all his cultivation of down-to-earth diction and familiar themes, he has always acknowledged the limitations of a purely neutral tone:

> Very little that catches the imagination can get clearance from either the intelligence or the moral sense. And equally, properly truthful or dispassionate themes enlist only the wannest support from the imagination. The poet is perpetually in that common human condition of trying to feel a thing because he believes it, or believe a thing because he feels it.[87]

It is what Larkin refers to here as 'the imagination' that frequently relies on symbolist strategies for its effects, although – presumably because unadulterated symbolism would be anathema to him – he has tended to deny this. Interestingly, a few of his earliest reviewers commented on it. In *The Times Literary Supplement*, for instance, *The Less Deceived* was said to have a 'sombrely tender vein reminiscent of Baudelaire, as in the poem "If, My Darling". The Baudelairean question "Vivrons-nous jamais?" haunts some of the finest poems in the book.'[88] John Wain made a similar judgement in a letter to the

London Magazine in 1957 about 'Church Going': 'in terms of ancestry, the central figure is descended from late nineteenth century poetry (Laforgue, Corbière), the intermediary being Mr Eliot's Prufrock.'[89] (Several years later, in *The Society of the Poem* (1971), Jonathan Raban was also to point out resemblances between Larkin's depressed, bicycle-clipped figure and Eliot's world-weary speaker. One might also add that Eliot's premature obsession with old age resembles Larkin's.) More recently, with a few shining exceptions, critics have tended to ignore or botch this aspect of Larkin's work, interpreting it, if at all, simply as allegory or metaphor. But Larkin has in fact stated clearly, if self-deprecatingly, that symbolism was important to him at least as a young man. Referring to his early writing, he has said that 'the real world was all right providing you made it pretty clear that it was a symbol';[90] and in one of his earliest published poems, 'Femmes Damnées' (written in 1943), the symbolist element is clearly apparent – though Larkin himself has disparagingly said 'The piece is evidence that I once read at least one "foreign poem" though I can't remember how far, if at all, my verses are based on the original'.[91] After describing one tousled, weeping woman, Rosemary, the poem turns to a second and ends:

> Stretched out before her, Rachel curls and curves,
> Eyelids and lips apart, her glances filled
> With satisfied ferocity; she smiles,
> As beasts smile on the prey they have just killed.
>
> The marble clock has stopped. The curtained sun
> Burns on: the room grows hot. There, it appears,
> A vase of flowers has spilt, and soaked away.
> The only sound heard is the sound of tears.[92]

It is in fact Baudelaire's 'Femmes Damnées' ('A la pâle clarté des lampes languissantes') that Larkin's poem echoes. Baudelaire's was originally intended for *Les Fleurs du Mal* but was removed on the insistence of the censor in 1857 and has subsequently been printed separately. Both poems describe two sensuously tragic lesbians (Baudelaire's are called Delphine and Hippolyte) and contain marked similarities of phrasing. The first stanza above, for instance, is based on the fourth of Baudelaire's:

> Étendue à ses pieds, calme et pleine de joie,
> Delphine la couvait avec des yeux ardents,
> Comme un animal fort qui surveille une proie,
> Après l'avoir d'abord marquée avec les dents.

Pointing out the resemblances between these two poems demolishes the popular belief that Larkin has never read or liked 'foreign poetry'. His three mature collections, of course, were all written after he had moderated his youthful interest in the symbolists, but it nevertheless asserts itself repeatedly and to considerable effect. Very occasionally, he has hinted at it: speaking on the radio in 1972, he admitted: 'What I should like to do is to write *different* kinds of poems, that might be by different people. Someone once said that the great thing is not to be different from other people, but to be different from yourself.'[93] He in fact manages this feat of transformation more often than his commentators are prepared to concede. Ten years earlier, for instance, he had said about his poem 'Absences': 'I fancy it sounds like a different, better poet than myself. The last line sounds like a slightly-unconvincing translation from a French Symbolist. I wish I could write like this more often.'[94]

> Rain patters on a sea that tilts and sighs.
> Fast-running floors, collapsing into hollows,
> Tower suddenly, spray-haired. Contrariwise,
> A wave drops like a wall: another follows,
> Wilting and scrambling, tirelessly at play
> Where there are no ships and no shallows.
>
> Above the sea, the yet more shoreless day,
> Riddled by wind, trails lit-up galleries:
> They shift to giant ribbing, sift away.
>
> Such attics cleared of me! Such absences! (*LD*, p. 40)

The energy of the descriptive language here anticipates a later poem – the second part of 'Livings' (HW, p. 14), which similarly begins from a naturalistic context and then makes excited leaps between ideas. In the first stanza of 'Absences' the sea's roughness turns waves from fluids to solids – from floors to hollows to towers to hair to a wall – as it mimes the processes of change and purgation experienced by the speaker. In the second stanza a similar transformation occurs 'Above the sea': the day 'trails' ships into the distance so that their natures are altered too. The final, isolated, triumphant line (Larkin later aimed for the same kind of exhilaration in 'The Card-Players') is a joyous assertion of the freedom this represents – not just from the potential distractions of human beings on their ships but from the stereotyped constraints imposed by a strictly empirical view of the world. The line also, appropriately, includes the poem's most radical imaginative jump – from sea to attics and from attics to absence itself – as well as raising to a climax the way in which the poem's language colludes with the theme of transformation. Its two phrases are a variation on a similar structure ('Such attics cleared of me' is recalled but contracted by 'Such absences'), just as the rhyme words, alliterations and echoes ('Riddled'/'ribbing', 'shift'/'sift') in previous lines all enact in linguistic terms the changes and alterations celebrated by the speaker.

The symbolist devices of 'Absences' allow Larkin to be unlike himself because they disrupt the normal relationships between concepts: by liberating him from the familiar, circumscribed world, they allow him to experience and convey a sense of transcendence. But this is not to say that disturbances of this sort always guarantee a positive and indubitable release. In 'Next, Please', for instance, the symbolist conclusion confirms the death-obsessed bleakness of the first five stanzas:

> Only one ship is seeking us, a black-
> Sailed unfamiliar, towing at her back
> A huge and birdless silence. In her wake
> No waters breed or break. (LD, p. 20)

These lines perfectly illustrate Yeats's contention that symbols intensify a poem's emotional charge. Although a metaphor of ships and sailing is developed throughout the poem, it is only in the last quatrain that the tone of rational argument and the structure of logical connections ('Always . . . Yet . . . But . . .') is exchanged for the more bizarre concentrations of symbolism proper (ships towing silence). The effect is movingly to confirm the fact and dread of death. There is, though, a sense in which the lines contain a saving grace, for all their denying any chance of actual salvation. They remove the speaker to a position outside familiar and familiarly threatening time because they release him from the world of ordinary events. As they do so, their expression of fear and awe is mitigated by a sense of the marvellous. The lines communicate an imaginative excitement which is at odds with the meaning they contain.

These compensatory effects are limited and provisional, but palpable. And, such as they are, they depend for much of their strength on being part of a dialogue: the rewards of their symbolist intensity are highlighted by the relative restraint of the first five stanzas. This point is confirmed by Larkin's most purely symbolist poem, 'Dry Point', where the lack of variety in tone and language emphasizes the speaker's preoccupation with being trapped. As he flickers from symbol to symbol, grappling with his horror of sexual disappointment, he finds only confirmation of losses, and proof that fulfilment is unobtainable:

> What ashen hills! what salted, shrunken lakes!
> How leaden the ring looks,
> Birmingham magic all discredited,
>
> And how remote that bare and sunscrubbed room,
> Intensely far, that padlocked cube of light
> We neither define nor prove,
> Where you, we dream, obtain no right of entry.
>
> (LD, p. 19)

There is no interaction here with straightforward, rational, logical progressions of images (and the obscurity of 'Birming-

76

ham magic' does not help: it refers to the fact that a particularly cheap and tawdry kind of wedding ring was produced in Birmingham). The result is a degree of uncertainty about the poem's direction, which confirms the speaker's isolation from the 'bare and sunscrubbed room' which is his goal. He is cut off from it not simply by the *tristesse* following sex but by an inability to 'define' and 'prove' the exact nature of his wants. His symbolist vagueness, in other words, is the cause of his predicament, as well as the means by which he expresses it.

Where 'Absences', say, or 'Coming', or even 'Next, Please' in its muted fashion, rise from observed and cramping familiars to a world of imaginative freedom, 'Dry Point' never escapes its own thwarting imprecisions. It is a revealing but untypical poem, and in the two collections he has published after the one in which it appears – *The Less Deceived* – he never again experimented so radically. In fact, had Larkin stopped writing after *The Whitsun Weddings*, it would have seemed that he had renounced symbolism altogether. Virtually all the poems in this second mature book are Hardyesque reflections, like 'Love Songs in Age', or extended metaphors, like 'Ambulances', or satires of self and society, like 'A Study of Reading Habits'. They are, of course, none the worse for being so – but it is an interesting point, in view of Larkin's supposed lack of development as a writer. *The Whitsun Weddings* is, to put it another way, the book that conforms most exactly to the attitudes and styles associated with the Movement. The Movement was first given popular definition almost exactly as Larkin finished *The Less Deceived*, and this seems to have hardened and accelerated his development towards an unmistakably English ideal. It is clear from the first part of this chapter that the most important and character-forming tensions in *The Whitsun Weddings* are between an undeceived pessimism and a wishful-thinking optimism – but these are seldom reflected in the crossing of two distinct styles and languages, as they are in *The Less Deceived* and *High Windows*.

There are, though, two poems in *The Whitsun Weddings* which show that Larkin did not abandon symbolism altogether during this period, but rather began a process of adaptation that is continued with greater urgency in *High Windows*. One of them is the title poem. Its grand finale is preceded by seven and a half stanzas of spacious, studied realism; it is a switch from one mode to another which recalls 'Absences' and 'Next, Please', but is more sudden and marked, and less obviously introduced by sympathetic metaphors:

> We slowed again,
> And as the tightening brakes took hold, there swelled
> A sense of falling, like an arrow-shower
> Sent out of sight, somewhere becoming rain. (WW, p. 23)

Here something potentially threatening is turned into something indispensable and nourishing. Arrows of conflict become – perhaps via an association with Blake's arrows of desire – Cupid's arrows, and during the process of transformation Larkin overcomes his sense of himself as an outsider. He is released from the empirically observed world, and its attendant disappointments, into one of transcendent imaginative fulfilment.

Much the same is true of 'Water', which demonstrates in miniature the same tactics as 'The Whitsun Weddings'. Its expositional opening ('If I were called in / To construct a religion / I should make use of water') introduces a metaphor which is gradually developed and intensified until the final stanza:

> And I should raise in the east
> A glass of water
> Where any-angled light
> Would congregate endlessly. (WW, p. 20)

The mundane glass of water becomes more than simply a sign and object of worship. It is transformed into an imaginative apprehension of endlessness, in which all knowledge of time and its constraints, and of self and its shortcomings, is set aside.

In *High Windows* the two sides of Larkin's literary personality are more sharply distinguished. The book contains more purely symbolist moments than *The Whitsun Weddings* ('So-lar', for instance, or 'Money'), and more freely imaginative narratives ('Livings', 'Dublinesque' and 'The Explosion'), but these things are offset by a more remorseless factuality, a greater crudity of language (in 'The Card-Players', for example), and an often blatantly simple pessimism ('Man hands on misery to man. / It deepens like a coastal shelf'; *HW*, p. 30). And as was the case in 'Next, Please' Larkin's exploitation of symbolist techniques does not always guarantee him absolute freedom from time and its ravages. At the end of 'Money', for instance, a gloomily rationalizing tone of voice is abandoned only to confirm despair:

> I listen to money singing. It's like looking down
> > From long french windows at a provincial town,
> The slums, the canal, the churches ornate and mad
> > In the evening sun. It is intensely sad. (*HW*, p. 40)

The visual freedom here, and the sense of being raised above immediate circumstances, cannot deny the force of the poem's final sentence. But, while it fails to liberate him from sadness altogether, 'Money' does draw attention to a recurrent and crucial feature of Larkin's symbolist innovations. They do not simply offer a potential consolation by representing a departure from the realistic mode which is associated with disappointment. They are nearly all, in one way or another, actually concerned with ideas of removal from the apparently inevitable frustrations that accompany rational discourse. Speech, at least notionally, is set aside in favour of sight – of 'looking down'. 'Solar' provides a more enduring release by the same means:

> The eye sees you
> Simplified by distance
> Into an origin,
> Your petalled head of flames
> Continuously exploding.
> Heat is the echo of your
> Gold. (*HW*, p. 33)

Here, as elsewhere, Larkin adopts the dislocations, illogicalities and imaginative excitement of symbolism to redeem himself from distressing daily circumstances. But his commitment to the real world is too great for him to achieve this kind of escape easily or often. Usually he creates an impression of release only to introduce a reminder of responsibilities as well. An earlier poem, 'Here', demonstrates that the very notion of distance is often regarded with ambivalence, whatever the style in which it is described. The advantages of remoteness are obvious: it means avoiding the shortcomings of others, if not of the self. It is for this reason, perhaps, that Larkin has always emphasized the isolation of the various places where he has lived. He has created a kind of private mythology, which in the case of Hull and Holderness has turned an admittedly cut-off district into a remote pastoral paradise:

> Here silence stands
> Like heat. Here leaves unnoticed thicken,
> Hidden weeds flower, neglected waters quicken,
> Luminously-peopled air ascends;
> And past the poppies bluish neutral distance
> Ends the land suddenly beyond a beach
> Of shapes and shingle. Here is unfenced existence:
> Facing the sun, untalkative, out of reach. (WW, p. 9)

The few people allowed into this personal Eden are reduced merely to 'shapes' – they are not enough to distract him from his silent self-forgetting. But the poem's final phrase – 'out of reach' – has an arresting ambiguity: the place is both beyond the reach of disturbances and also beyond his reach. It is both 'Here' and nowhere, and attainable only in imagination, not in fact. While this emphasizes its privacy, it also hints at a disadvantage: the evocation of distance allows freedom from self, people and time, but it simultaneously denies the theoretical and sometimes necessary support of company. It also, in its neutral vacancy, prefigures the inevitable emptiness of death.

Precisely this tension recurs in the poem of Larkin's which

most successfully employs symbolist techniques, 'High Windows'. For its first four verses, he creates a persona who is angrily disappointed that promises made to him as a young man have not been fulfilled. But as he speculates about the new generation's chances of happiness he realizes that he might once have been similarly envied. The cycle of time brings round hope and frustration ceaselessly, and no one – to extricate a phrase buried in the image of 'an outdated combine harvester' – gets their oats. As so often in his other poems, the wasted opportunities of the past and the exclusions of the future coalesce to tyrannize the present. But here they provoke a conclusion that contains some hope of reprieve:

> Rather than words comes the thought of high windows:
> The sun-comprehending glass,
> And beyond it, the deep blue air, that shows
> Nothing, and is nowhere, and is endless. (*HW*, p. 17)

The most obvious reward of this 'thought' is that it removes him from the context of actual human fallibility. It is an exalted imaginative alternative – in secular terms – to the false 'paradise' of sexual freedom and godless independence promised on earth. But clearly there are drawbacks. As the speaker imagines himself staring out through the divisive 'sun-comprehending glass' (it recalls Shelley's 'dome of many-coloured glass' between life and death) he cannot entirely suppress the effect of the two negatives 'Nothing' and 'nowhere'. For all their freedom from specific circumstances, they imply extinction. Like the 'unfenced existence' of 'Here', the 'deep blue air' of 'High Windows' reminds him of his commitment to the world. It does so, moreover, by a shift from grumbling, ironical, colloquial speech to symbolist intensity which both illustrates Larkin's mastery of poetic tones and – as in 'Money' and 'Solar' – undermines the notion of the poem as a verbal device altogether. The final lines are offered 'Rather than words'. Obviously they are words – how else could the poem exist? – but it is a crucial part of their function to convey an inexpressible element in the thought they contain.

For all their variety, the methods that Larkin adopts in his pursuit of happiness have at least one thing in common. They suggest – and often actually state – that his ideal is at best elusive and at worst illusory. The only thing he can hope for is a temporary reprieve from a pervasive sense of his own failure, and the ubiquitous evidence of other people's absurdity or self-deception. But, while it is often snubbed, his hope is resolute, and in a very large number of poems it leads him to create a dialogue between opposing attitudes: sociability and singleness, work and idleness, resolution and despair. Invariably, the thwarting, negative side of the argument emerges as the strongest – but this does not mean that Larkin is incapable of finding consolations and satisfactions in existence.

The same life-enhancing struggle between opposites is evident in the style and language of his work. His original admiration for the heroic, aspiring, self-dramatizing characteristics of Yeats was not completely dispelled as his sympathy for the humbler manner of the English line developed: it was restrained and made to perform a crucial role in the creation of his mature style. Even in the poems that adopt primarily Hardyesque neutral tones, there are frequent flashes of rhetoric which recall Yeats's grander manner. The result is a number of poems that emerge as 'rhetorically persuasive' Yeatsian affirmations, [and] do not disregard the difficulties but hold them magnificently at bay from some superior inch of imaginative height'.[95] Saying so involves contradicting several of Larkin's own resonant self-analyses, as well as several of his commentators' judgements of his unflinching pessimism. Revealingly, though, he opened *The Less Deceived* with a poem, 'Lines on a Young Lady's Photograph Album', which expressly states the losses of a narrowly literal attitude to experience. Photography, the poem says, depends for its charm and successes on depicting 'real' people in a 'real' place, and on being 'in every sense empirically true'. But it is exactly for these reasons that Larkin will not accord it the status of 'art' – which, he implies, depends on allowing the imagination free and potentially transfiguring play. It is a characteristically ambivalent poem – a showpiece of the Movement, but discreetly hinting at the Movement's limitations. His three mature collections have developed attitudes and styles of greater imaginative daring: in their prolonged debates with despair, they testify to wide sympathies, contain passages of frequently transcendent beauty, and demonstrate a poetic inclusiveness which is of immense consequence for his literary heirs.

NOTES

1 Philip Larkin, 'The Pleasure Principle', *Listen*, 2 (Summer–Autumn 1957), p. 29.
2 Philip Larkin, 'Speaking of Writing: XIII', *The Times*, 20 February 1964, p. 16.
3 Philip Larkin, 'Big Victims', *New Statesman*, 13 March 1970, p. 368.
4 W. B. Yeats, 'The Symbolism of Poetry', *Essays and Introductions* (London: Macmillan, 1969), p. 157.
5 Ibid., p. 156.
6 Quoted in Edmund Wilson, *Axel's Castle*, 5th impression (London: Fontana, 1969), p. 23.
7 See Yeats, op. cit., p. 163.
8 See Barbara Everett, 'Philip Larkin: After Symbolism', *Essays in Criticism*, 30, 3 (July 1980), pp. 231–8.
9 'Four Conversations: Philip Larkin' (interviewer Ian Hamilton), *London Magazine*, 4, 8 (November 1964), p. 73.
10 T. S. Eliot, 'Tradition and the Individual Talent', *Selected Essays*, 3rd enlarged edn (London: Faber, 1951), p. 13.
11 *The New Poetry*, ed. A. Alvarez (Harmondsworth: Penguin, 1962), p. 22.
12 Donald Davie, *Thomas Hardy and British Poetry* (London: Routledge & Kegan Paul, 1973), p. 12.
13 'Four Conversations', p. 71.
14 David Timms, *Philip Larkin* (Edinburgh: Oliver & Boyd, 1973), p. 67.
15 Philip Larkin, 'Wanted: Good Hardy Critic', *Critical Quarterly*, 8, 2 (Summer 1966), p. 174.
16 'Four Conversations', p. 71.
17 Quoted in *Poets of the 1950s*, ed. D. J. Enright (Tokyo: Kenkyusha Press, 1955), p. 78.
18 'Four Conversations', p. 71.

19 Edna Longley, 'Larkin, Edward Thomas and the Tradition', *Phoenix* (Philip Larkin Issue), 11–12 (Autumn and Winter 1973–4), p. 64.

20 'A Poet on the 8.15' (interviewer John Horder), *The Guardian*, 20 May 1965, p. 9.

21 J. R. Watson, 'The Other Larkin', *Critical Quarterly*, 17, 4 (Winter 1975), p. 354.

22 'The Unsung Gold Medallist' (interviewer Philip Oakes), *Sunday Times Magazine*, 27 March 1966, p. 65.

23 Ibid.

24 'Four Young Poets, I: Philip Larkin', *The Times Educational Supplement*, 2147 (13 July 1956), p. 933.

25 Alan Brownjohn, *Philip Larkin*, Writers and their Work, No. 247 (London: Longman, 1975), p. 4.

26 Philip Larkin, 'Not the Place's Fault', *Umbrella*, 1, 3 (Summer 1959), p. 109.

27 Ibid.

28 Quoted in Blake Morrison, *The Movement* (London: Oxford University Press, 1980), p. 15.

29 'Four Young Poets', p. 933.

30 Ibid.

31 'A Sharp-Edged View' (interviewer Frances Hill), *The Times Educational Supplement*, 2974 (19 May 1972), p. 19.

32 *The Arts Council Collection of Modern Literary Manuscripts 1963–1972*, ed. Jenny Stratford, Preface by Philip Larkin (London: Turret Books, 1974), p. 20.

33 Martin Dodsworth (ed.), *The Survival of Poetry* (London: Faber, 1970), p. 42.

34 Quoted in Morrison, op. cit., p. 27.

35 'A Sharp-edged View', p. 19.

36 Information supplied by The Brynmor Jones Library, University of Hull.

37 'A Sharp-Edged View', p. 19.

38 Larkin, 'Not the Place's Fault', p. 111.

39 *The Times Literary Supplement*, 13 April 1973, p. 406.

40 'A Great Parade of Single Poems: Interview with Anthony Thwaite', *The Listener*, 12 April 1973, p. 473.

41 The author was J. D. Scott, literary editor of the *Spectator*.

42 *Spectator*, 1 October 1954, p. 400.

43 D. J. Enright's *Poets of the 1950s* included poems by Enright, Amis, Conquest, Davie, Hollander, Jennings, Larkin and Wain.

44 *New Lines*, ed. Robert Conquest (London: Macmillan, 1956), pp. xiv–xv.

45 Ibid., p. xv.
46 Donald Davie, *Purity of Diction in English Verse* (London: Chatto & Windus, 1952), p. 52.
47 Quoted in Morrison, op. cit., p. 60.
48 *The New Poetry*, p. 25.
49 Morrison, op. cit., p. 120.
50 Ibid., p. 117.
51 Quoted in ibid., p. 117.
52 Brownjohn, op. cit., p. 6.
53 'Four Conversations', p. 72.
54 Quoted in Timms, op. cit., p. 55.
55 'Philip Larkin Praises the Poetry of Thomas Hardy', *The Listener*, 25 July 1968, p. 11.
56 Timms, op. cit., p. 35.
57 Clive James, *At the Pillars of Hercules* (London: Faber, 1979), p. 69.
58 In Dodsworth, op. cit., p. 48.
59 Longley, op. cit., p. 81.
60 In Dodsworth, op. cit., p. 50.
61 'A Conversation with Philip Larkin', *Tracks*, 1 (Summer 1967), p. 9.
62 'Four Conversations', p. 75.
63 Ibid.
64 Larkin, 'The Pleasure Principle', p. 29.
65 'A Conversation with Philip Larkin', p. 10.
66 Timms, op. cit., p. 37.
67 Philip Larkin, *Jill* (London: Fortune Press, 1946), p. 133.
68 Ibid.
69 John Haffenden, *Viewpoints: Poets in Conversation* (London: Faber, 1981), p. 116.
70 John Bayley, *The Uses of Division* (London: Chatto & Windus, 1976), p. 170.
71 See Bruce K. Martin, *Philip Larkin* (Boston, Mass.: Twayne, 1978), p. 119.
72 Eric Homberger, *The Art of the Real* (London: Dent, 1977), p. 74.
73 Geoffrey Thurley, *The Ironic Harvest* (London: Arnold, 1974), p. 145.
74 Charles Tomlinson, 'The Middlebrow Muse', *Essays in Criticism*, 7, 2 (April 1957), p. 214.
75 'A Conversation with Philip Larkin', p. 8.
76 Larkin, 'Wanted: Good Hardy Critic', p. 178.
77 'Four Conversations', p. 73.
78 *The Times Literary Supplement*, 23 December 1977, p. 1491.
79 Donald Davie, 'Remembering the Movement', in Barry Alpert

(ed.), *The Poet in the Imaginary Museum* (Manchester: Carcanet, 1977), p. 75.

80 Actually the holding hands are a nineteenth-century addition.

81 Martin, op. cit., p. 90.

82 Timms, op. cit., p. 64.

83 James, op. cit., p. 54.

84 'Four Conversations', p. 73.

85 *The Times Literary Supplement*, 23 December 1977, p. 1491.

86 Larkin, 'Wanted: Good Hardy Critic', p. 178.

87 'Context: Philip Larkin', *London Magazine*, 1, 11 (February 1962), p. 32.

88 Review of *The Less Deceived, The Times Literary Supplement*, 16 December 1955, p. 762.

89 John Wain, letter to the *London Magazine* (March 1957), p. 56.

90 'A Conversation with Philip Larkin', p. 7.

91 Philip Larkin, *Femmes Damnées*, Sycamore Broadsheet 27 (Oxford: Sycamore Press, 1978).

92 Ibid.

93 Quoted in Timms, op. cit., p. 121.

94 Philip Larkin, in Paul Engle and Joseph Langland (eds), *Poet's Choice* (New York: Dial Press, 1962), p. 202.

95 Longley, op. cit., p. 87.

BIBLIOGRAPHY

WORKS BY PHILIP LARKIN

Manuscripts

Manuscript notebook (5 October 1944–10 March 1950), containing autograph drafts and revisions of about eighty-five poems. Presented to the British Library Department of Manuscripts for the Arts Council Collection of Modern Literary Manuscripts. Add. MS 52,619.

Jill. London: Fortune Press, 1946. Printer's copy for Faber edition published in 1964. Presented by Philip Larkin to the Bodleian Library, Oxford, on 21 April 1965. Arch. AA e 86.

Poetry collections

The North Ship. London: Fortune Press, 1945. 2nd edn, introduced by Philip Larkin, with an additional poem taken from *XX Poems.* London and Boston, Mass.: Faber, 1966.

XX Poems. Privately printed in a limited edition of 100 copies. Belfast, 1951.

The Fantasy Poets: Philip Larkin. Swineford: Fantasy Press, 1954.

The Less Deceived. London: Marvell Press, 1955.

The Whitsun Weddings. London and Boston, Mass.: Faber, 1964.

High Windows. London: Faber, 1974. New York: Farrar, Straus & Giroux, 1974.

Femmes Damnées. Sycamore Broadsheet 27. Oxford: Sycamore Press, 1978.

Novels

Jill. London: Fortune Press, 1946. 2nd edn, introduced by Philip Larkin. London: Faber, 1964. 1st paperback edn. London: Faber, 1975. New York: Overlook Press, 1976.

88

A Girl in Winter. London: Faber, 1947. 1st paperback edn. London: Faber, 1975. New York: Overlook Press, 1976.

Prose non-fiction

All What Jazz: A Record Diary 1961–68. London: Faber, 1970. New York: St Martin's Press, 1970.

Works edited, or with contributions, by Philip Larkin

Oxford Poetry 1942–1943. Ed. Ian Davie. Oxford: Blackwell, 1943.
Poetry from Oxford in Wartime. Ed. William Bell. London: Fortune Press, 1945.
Poets of the 1950s. Ed. D. J. Enright. Tokyo: Kenkyusha Press, 1955.
New Lines. Ed. Robert Conquest. London: Macmillan, 1956.
Poet's Choice. Ed. Paul Engle and Joseph Langland. (Contains 'Absences' and an explanatory note.) New York: Dial Press, 1962.
The Oxford Book of Twentieth-Century English Verse. Ed. Philip Larkin. Oxford: Clarendon Press, 1973.
The Arts Council Collection of Modern Literary Manuscripts 1963–1972. A catalogue edited by Jenny Stratford, with a Preface by Philip Larkin. London: Turret Books, 1974.

Uncollected criticism and essays

'The Writer in His Age: Philip Larkin'. *London Magazine*, 4 (May 1957).
'The Pleasure Principle'. *Listen*, 2 (Summer–Autumn 1957).
'Betjeman En Bloc'. *Listen*, 3 (Spring 1959).
'The Savage Seventh'. *Spectator*, 20 November 1959.
'Not the Place's Fault'. *Umbrella*, 1, 3 (Summer 1959).
'Context: Philip Larkin'. *London Magazine*, 1, 11 (February 1962).
'The Poetry of William Barnes'. *The Listener*, 16 August 1962.
'Wanted: Good Hardy Critic'. *Critical Quarterly*, 8, 2 (Summer 1966).
'Philip Larkin Praises the Poetry of Thomas Hardy'. *The Listener*, 25 July 1968.
'Big Victims: Emily Dickinson and Walter de la Mare'. *New Statesman*, 13 March 1970.
'Stevie, Good-bye'. *The Observer*, 23 January 1972.
'The Hidden Hardy'. *New Statesman*, 2 June 1972.
'The State of Poetry – A Symposium: Philip Larkin'. *The Review*, 29–30 (Spring–Summer 1972).

'Worksheets of "At Grass"'. *Phoenix*, 11–12 (Autumn and Winter 1973–4).
'The Real Wilfred: Owen's Life and Legends'. *Encounter*, 44 (March 1975).

Interviews

'Four Young Poets, I: Philip Larkin'. *The Times Educational Supplement*, 2147 (13 July 1956).
'Speaking of Writing: XIII'. *The Times*, 20 February 1964.
'Four Conversations' (interviewer Ian Hamilton). *London Magazine*, 4, 8 (November 1964).
'A Poet on the 8.15' (interviewer John Horder). *The Guardian*, 20 May 1968.
'The Unsung Gold Medallist' (interviewer Philip Oakes). *Sunday Times Magazine*, 27 March 1966.
'A Conversation with Philip Larkin'. *Tracks*, 1 (Summer 1967).
'A Sharp-Edged View' (interviewer Frances Hill). *The Times Educational Supplement*, 2974 (19 May 1972).
'A Great Parade of Single Poems: Interview with Anthony Thwaite'. *The Listener*, 12 April 1973.
'Philip Larkin – A Profile' (interviewer Dan Jacobson). *The New Review*, 1, 3 (June 1974).
'A Voice for our Time' (interviewer Miriam Gross). *The Observer*, 16 December 1979.
Haffenden, John (ed.). *Viewpoints: Poets in Conversation*. London: Faber, 1981.

BIBLIOGRAPHY

Bloomfield, B. C. *Philip Larkin: A Bibliography*. London: Faber, 1980.

SELECTED CRITICISM OF PHILIP LARKIN

Books

Brownjohn, Alan. *Philip Larkin*. Writers and their Work, No. 247. London: Longman for the British Council, 1975.
Kuby, Lolette. *Philip Larkin: An Uncommon Poet for the Common Man*. The Hague: Mouton, 1974.
Martin, Bruce K. *Philip Larkin*. Boston, Mass.: Twayne, 1978.
Timms, David. *Philip Larkin*. Edinburgh: Oliver & Boyd, 1973.

Selected articles

Alvarez, A. 'Verse Chronicle: Philip Larkin'. In *Beyond All This Fiddle*, pp. 85–7. London: Allen Lane, 1968.

Bateson, F. W. 'Auden's (and Empson's) Heirs'. *Essays in Criticism*, 7 (January 1957).

Bedient, Calvin. 'Philip Larkin'. In *Eight Contemporary Poets*, pp. 69–94. London: Oxford University Press, 1974.

Chambers, Harry. 'The Poetry of Philip Larkin'. *Phoenix*, 9 (Summer 1963).

Davie, Donald. 'Landscapes of Larkin'. In *Thomas Hardy and British Poetry*, pp. 63–82. London: Routledge & Kegan Paul, 1973.

—— 'Remembering the Movement'. In Barry Alpert (ed.), *The Poet in the Imaginary Museum*, pp. 72–5. Manchester: Carcanet, 1977.

Enright, D. J. 'Down Cemetery Road'. In *Conspirators and Poets*, pp. 141–6. London: Chatto & Windus, 1966.

Everett, Barbara. 'Larkin's Edens'. *English* (Spring 1982).

—— 'Philip Larkin: After Symbolism'. *Essays in Criticism*, 30, 3 (July 1980).

Falck, Colin. 'Philip Larkin'. In Ian Hamilton (ed.), *The Modern Poet: Essays from 'The Review'*. London: Macdonald, 1968.

Gardner, Philip. 'The Wintry Drum: The Poetry of Philip Larkin'. *Dalhousie Review*, 48, 1 (September 1968).

Gindin, James. 'The First Steps'. In *Postwar British Fiction: New Accents and Attitudes*, pp. 1–2. Cambridge: Cambridge University Press, 1962.

Hamilton, Ian. 'The Making of the Movement'. *New Statesman*, 23 April 1971.

Homberger, Eric. 'The 1950s'. In *The Art of the Real*, pp. 70–80; and *passim*. London: Dent, 1977.

James, Clive. 'Don Juan in Hull'. In *At the Pillars of Hercules*, pp. 51–72. London: Faber, 1979.

Lehmann, John. 'The Wain–Larkin Myth'. *The Sewanee Review*, 66, 4 (Autumn 1958).

Morrison, Blake. In *The Movement: British Poetry and Fiction of the 1950s, passim*. London: Oxford University Press, 1980.

O'Connor, William van. 'The Quiet Poem'. In *The New University Wits and the End of Modernism*, pp. 16–29. Carbondale, Ill.: Southern Illinois University Press, 1963.

Phoenix, 11–12 (Autumn and Winter 1973–4). Philip Larkin Issue.

Press, John. 'The Movement' and 'Poets of the 1950s'. In *A Map of Modern English Verse*, pp. 203–14, 251–61. London: Oxford University Press, 1969.

Ricks, Christopher. 'The Words and Music of Life'. *The Sunday Times*, 7 January 1968.

Rosenthal, M. L. 'Robert Lowell and the Poetry of Confusion'. In *The Modern Poets: A Critical Introduction*, pp. 222–4. New York: Oxford University Press, 1960.

Thurley, Geoffrey. 'The Legacy of Auden'. In *The Ironic Harvest*, pp. 141–9. London: Arnold, 1974.

Thwaite, Anthony. 'The Poetry of Philip Larkin'. In Martin Dodsworth (ed.), *The Survival of Poetry*. London: Faber, 1970.

—— In *Poetry Today: 1900–1970*, pp. 33–6. London: Longman for the British Council, 1973.

Tomlinson, Charles. 'The Middlebrow Muse'. *Essays in Criticism*, 7, 2 (April 1957).

Wain, John. 'Engagement or Withdrawal?'. *Critical Quarterly*, 6, 2 (Summer 1964).

—— 'A Literary Chapter'. In *Sprightly Running*, pp. 187–8. London: Macmillan, 1962.

Watson, J. R. 'The Other Larkin'. *Critical Quarterly*, 17, 4 (Winter 1975).